MW00611267

"Carolina Gelen's debut cookbook is packed full of real recipes for real life, each bursting with the warmth you know and love her for. There are so many smart dishes using simple ingredients in ingenious ways that I don't even know where to start! Now's our chance to hang out in the kitchen with our favorite social media friend."

—**Sohla El-Waylly,** *New York Times* bestselling author of *Start Here*

"Carolina's *Pass the Plate* is a must-have for all food lovers. Her talent shines on every page of the book as she brings exciting, innovative ideas and flavor to the table. Carolina's recipes are unique, yet she keeps the recipes highly approachable and extremely cookable for all levels of cooks. I am certain that readers will fall in love with cooking all over again as they cook their way through Carolina's first masterpiece."

—**Alex Snodgrass,** *New York Times* bestselling author and creator of *The Defined Dish*

"Carolina's like your favorite cooking teacher, bringing warmth and expertise into your kitchen. With a focus on doable yet extraordinary recipes, she unlocks a world of flavor you never knew existed."

—**Hannah Neeleman** of Ballerina Farm

"In a world where many people just do the same thing over and over again, Carolina Gelen, her recipes, and now her debut cookbook do the exact opposite. I am constantly blown away not only by her creativity but also by how each and every recipe I've made from her is perfectly done. Her flavor combinations are unmatched. Her techniques are flawless. Her imagination knows no bounds. I would do anything to be her neighbor. Trust me when I tell you that this book will be your new favorite!"

—**Gaby Dalkin,** *New York Times* bestselling author and founder of *What's Gaby Cooking*

"Not a lot of cookbooks make me shouty, but this one did instantly: Everything looks so good! It's clever, innovative, and fresh, I hardly know what to cook first."

—**Deb Perelman,** author of *Smitten Kitchen Keepers*

"*Pass the Plate* offers a glimpse into the mastermind of Carolina Gelen I've been waiting for—and it's everything I hoped it would be. Her passion, grit, and love for food melt off each page, and the recipes are a rare and welcome combination of simple and drool-worthy. I can't wait to make every single one!"

—**Melissa Ben-Ishay,** *New York Times* bestselling author and creator of *Baked by Melissa*

Pass the Plate

Pass *the* Plate

100 Delicious, Highly Shareable, Everyday Recipes

Carolina Gelen

Photographs by Nico Schinco

Clarkson Potter/Publishers | **New York**

I dedicate this cookbook to my wonderful community and all who've welcomed it into their kitchens. I hope these recipes nourish your soul, satiate your hunger, and leave a smile on your face. Thank you from the bottom of my heart for allowing me to be a part of your world.

CONTENTS

169
soup's on

187
salad days

211
side dish savvy

237
sweets & treats

In Romania, though I was an only child, I grew up in a large family, surrounded by lots of loud aunts, uncles, and a bunch of cousins who were like my siblings.

When we'd get together, the room would instantly become super loud, but as soon as the food got to the table, it would create a sense of calmness. The aroma of the food was so inviting and comforting, whispering at us to enjoy life. We'd set up these big pots and pans of chicken soup, roast chicken, mici (Romanian flavored meat rolls), couscous, and cabbage rolls, plus all the accompaniments—so many homemade pickles, marinated roasted peppers, fresh bread, piles of fresh scallions, raw garlic cloves, chiles, and dips. The person closest to the food would plate everyone's meal, telling everyone at the table to "pass the plate" so they could fill it for them.

I wanted to channel that spirit of good food and family here in my first cookbook, filling it with recipes that are so delicious but easy to make, using ingredients you probably already have.

Whatever life throws at you, I created these recipes to be accessible, tasty, and nourishing—for yourself, as well as your loved ones.

I hope this becomes a cookbook you can count on for any occasion, from a late-night snack emergency, a special anniversary, a breakfast gathering, to a cozy Wednesday night in.

The food in this book is a diverse collection, drawing from my immigrant background, including living in Transylvania for most of my life, moving to the US, where I became familiar with classic American foods, and working in various professional kitchens with so many talented folks. You'll find American classics with unique twists and upgrades, such as my rich and creamy Brie mac and cheese with garlicky panko, alongside nostalgic Eastern European dishes I crave when I'm missing home, like my garlicky one-pan chicken couscous or ginormous cabbage roll cake. You'll also find fun dishes born of letting loose in the kitchen and being creative and resourceful, like my crispy ketchup rice for breakfast or a humble no-bake salted milk chocolate pie.

I believe cooking should be an enjoyable experience, not some stressful task you always postpone. With these highly doable recipes, I want you to feel comfortable in the kitchen, regardless of your background or skill level. With this in mind, most recipes in the cookbook use pantry-friendly, humble ingredients that you can find in most grocery stores across the country and are as stress-free and flexible as possible. I made it a point to make my instructions thorough and the design easy to follow along.

There's truly something for everyone, and I can't wait to see what you find for yourself and make your own. My dream is that *Pass the Plate* will live on your kitchen counter, developing so many creases and grease stains because it's so well-loved that you come back to it repeatedly, enjoying recipe after recipe. If this cookbook keeps you inspired, satisfied, and brings you closer to your community, I have fulfilled my biggest goal. I hope you will love the food so much that you can't help but ask for seconds and pass the plate to the person next to you.

food and family: from romania to america

As soon as I had a slight interest in cooking, my mother allowed me to be in the kitchen with her at every single step.

My father would sweat while he watched his five-year-old hold a paring knife and would anxiously yell the forty-seven ways the knife could fall and stab me, but my parents still somehow allowed me to always join them in the kitchen. My mother never followed recipes, and picking up her resourcefulness and make-it-your-own attitude has helped me through my cooking journey. While I was fortunate enough to later work in restaurants from a bagel shop to a luxury resort with a James Beard Award–winning chef, the most significant impact on my cooking was my mother.

One particular memory stands out for me. Every week when I was growing up, my mother would have a donut day—in Romania we call donuts gogoşi (pronounced go-go-shee), so technically, it was a gogoşi day. She'd make the dough from scratch, always without a measuring cup or scale in sight. She'd take out this giant stainless steel bowl and start by crumbling a fresh yeast block in—I can still smell that scent perfuming our kitchen—followed by lots of sugar and milk. Then I'd get to mix in the flour or whatever else she'd hand me—messy business, such a thrill for any child. She'd place her red and white plaid tablecloth over the dough to cover it while proofing. My mother never used tablecloths for setting up the table, so whenever I'd see that cloth pictured in the image below pulled out of the cabinet, I knew it could mean only one thing: It's donut day. She would then wrap the dough in two wool blankets and place it next to the warm radiator to proof. Once it was ready, we'd roll out the dough and start cutting it into circles using this floral mug that had the perfect donut diameter.

While my mother would be in charge of this task, she'd pass me a quarter of the dough and let me play with it, cutting out all these funky shapes with a tiny paring knife. The concept of proofing meant nothing to me back then, so I'd knead the dough again, messing up its rise, so much so that my donuts would always end up dense and heavy. I never understood why hers were always better than mine—until I did!

After frying the donuts to golden crisp perfection, we'd move on to grinding the sugar. My mother would use this tiny twenty-year-old coffee grinder to make powdered sugar by simply blending granulated sugar. I still remember the aroma when she opened the tight lid to the powdered sugar: a cloud of it would flood the air. We'd toss it in a big plastic bag, then add the freshly fried donuts, twisting the end of the bag and shaking hard to coat the donuts in sugar. Now imagine the joy in the eyes of a five-year-old seeing a dozen donuts dumped in a stainless steel bowl, just for them. My mother would place the bowl in my lap as I turned on my favorite cartoons.

I also remember the first time my mother allowed me to bake all by myself and use the oven for the first time. I must've been six or seven when I made poppy seed–coated pretzel bagels, following this obscure online recipe. Of course, I forgot the salt in the dough and they ended up a little bland, but we still enjoyed them and shared them with our neighbors across the hallway. I had developed a passion, and as I got older, cooking was the only hobby that stuck with me. I learned to make progress, not perfection. By the age of twelve, I was making fancy croquembouches and homemade croissants.

As my skills in the kitchen grew, I wanted to expand my repertoire beyond the classic Romanian and Hungarian foods I grew up with. We didn't have much and going to restaurants was a once-a-year treat, so my mother and I would watch *MasterChef*, Jamie Oliver, Anna Olsen, Nigella Lawson, Yotam Ottolenghi, and other talented chefs, and try to replicate the dishes we saw them make.

As my passion grew, I often found myself in the middle of Transylvania, trying to reproduce recipes from my favorite TV chefs and bakers but not able to find ingredients, such as canned pumpkin puree or cranberry sauce, sweetened condensed milk, or those white marshmallows you see in s'mores (the most common marshmallow option where I'm from is a pale pink and yellow marshmallow swirl). I had to learn to make all those things myself from scratch.

Watching those chefs helped my family and me expand our palates and explore new cuisines. To this day, even though my parents don't speak English, they understand the language of food when I share my recipes and videos online, thus supporting the concept that food is a universal language, transcending cultures and unifying people.

One thing that fascinated me about the TV chefs was all the glass bowls they used for their mise en place. So on Sundays, we would often go to a local flea market to look for glass bowls for my imaginary cooking show—I was constantly narrating my steps out loud with each dish I was cooking. Years later, I still find one of the biggest cooking inspirations to be thrift shopping. When you find a unique antique dish in a thrift store or at a flea market that speaks to you—whether you're attracted to its color, texture, or overall design—there's something so inspiring about the backstories you envision. And it's always fun to imagine how this new find will be featured, from the star at a dinner party to a vessel for sweet treats after lunch.

With all this passion for cooking, you might think I was hoping to make a career of it, to become a chef and start a restaurant, but you'd be wrong. Growing up in an Eastern European home after your parents suffered through communism, dictators, and poverty, you're taught the way to escape this cycle is to go to college and get a white-collar job. (Once, when I was visiting Romania after returning from the States, I ran into a former teacher who, after I told her I worked in food, replied, "But I thought you were smart!") In this culture, you're encouraged to become a doctor, a lawyer, an engineer, or a computer programmer to make your family proud and escape to something better. You're reminded of what they endured and taught through stories. One story my parents told me has stuck with me. Under the Romanian dictator Ceauşescu, my parents were given a bag of oranges every year during wintertime. Oranges were such a rare and special thing and they had so little, they would eat the entire orange, even the peels. We take such a simple thing like an orange for granted now, but it was a scarce treat in those days. Nowadays, my family skips eating orange peels, but will still save them and dry them on the radiator as a bittersweet memory of the past.

So under the circumstances, turning my cooking hobby into a career was never even a thought. Instead, I followed the path I was supposed to follow: I went to college to study computer science. It wasn't something I was particularly passionate about, and looking back, I only convinced myself I was enjoying it. The way I looked at it, it was a bachelor program that would guarantee me a decent job after I finished and provide a path to support myself and a way to escape the poverty of the past.

A few months into my first semester, I became convinced this wasn't for me. I had no joy learning about computer parts, freaky-funky math, and finding solutions for algorithmic problems I never cared for in the first place. Algorithms were quite fun to learn about, until they quickly turned not-so-fun and too complex for my liking.

Long story short, I knew it wasn't for me from the start, but there was one big problem: I didn't want to let my parents down. As the first person in my family to go to college, with that opportunity, quitting was never an option. I was unhappy, but not knowing what else to do, I was stuck, and suffered through it. An important thing I learned in college was that the smartest students were the ones most passionate about the subject. Their passions lived both inside and outside the classroom and they thrived.

Feeling so unhappy, and jealous of those who so loved this thing I hated and struggled to enjoy, I made a decision. The minute the semester ended, while my fellow computer science classmates were enrolling in summer internships, I applied for a program that would get me a summer job in the United States. Not any job, a job in a restaurant, which was my ultimate dream! I applied for a J-1 visa, created to expose foreigners to the United States culture and institutions through educational exchange work programs. You get to work in the United States for a set amount of time, travel, and return home with some memories and experiences.

I first came to the United States in the summer of 2018 and I loved it so much I went back again the following year. I worked in Park City, Utah, a resort town where there's never a dull moment or a shortage of people wanting good food. Both times I took on two jobs, working sixteen-hour days, getting maybe four or six hours of sleep a night. I was like a sponge, soaking it all up. It wasn't work to me, but a labor of love. I loved getting up in the morning, cooking, interacting with customers, it was such a thrill! I worked in multiple spots, from a bagel shop and a farm-to-table luxury restaurant to a brewery pub restaurant. I was finally in my element, like a fish in water.

After my second summer in Utah ended, the program was over and I had to return to college in Romania. There, I struggled my way through the work, with lots of tears and frustrations. At the time, I was renting a room for $150 a month from this old couple who had a small kitchen, plus it came with a friendly dog in the house. The only thing I looked forward to was coming home, cooking, and sitting on the porch while the dog, Azorel, waited for some food to fall on the ground. The meals didn't need to be unique to comfort me—sometimes it was a fifteen-minute garlic pasta, a basic root vegetable salad, or simply adding garlic, parsley, and hot sauce to a pack of instant noodles.

At the end of the semester, I had to get an internship in a computer programming field to complete my degree. While still in my college town, I enrolled in a German automotive company's program and had the thrilling job of programming car parts. I came home every day more depressed than ever, and again looked forward only to cooking a fun meal for dinner as a distraction from being so miserable. I'd cook anything from a slow-cooked lentil stew, a from-scratch chicken ramen, a full-on chicken roast, to sixteen-hour veggie burgers.

In the US, I worked two restaurant jobs for sixteen hours straight but felt exhilarated and alive with passion, while working eight hours programming car parts left me feeling empty and drained. My body may have been trapped in a mandatory internship for eight hours, but my heart was dreaming of food. That is when I started regularly posting my meals online on my Instagram account.

I didn't think much of it then, but one day, styling and shooting a video of a simple salad I had thrown together for lunch sparked something in me, so much so that from then on, I didn't go a meal without posting it online. I didn't know anything about shooting videos or styling food and props. I taught myself through trial and error and constantly worked to improve each of my creations. I never knew you could make a career by shooting food online. I just kept doing it simply for the passion and joy of it and eventually people started paying attention.

Then to my surprise, after a few months of sharing my food and online recipes, the *New York Times Cooking* social media manager reached out to me with an email, gauging my interest in producing a few videos for them. It was shocking to say the least, but it was the biggest compliment and I felt so much joy. Creating content for them was something I looked forward to, it felt like a treat every single time, not once like work.

No more than three months later, I was asked to join the Food52 recipe developer team. I still remember the thrill I felt the first time Food52 reshared one of my creations, so to have them reach out with this felt surreal. Of course, I said yes and took this on as well.

This was the first time I thought "There might be something here." If before, I couldn't envision a career in it, these two incredible blessings opened my eyes to new opportunities. Maybe I could build a career in doing something I love. Do you mean to tell me I can get paid to do something I have been doing for free for years? Sign me up! From there I started sharing more and more recipes while growing a wonderful online community of cooking enthusiasts.

To facilitate this, I emigrated to the US mid-Covid, starting a life here as I outgrew my small town in Romania to make my dream of cooking into a successful career. I never envisioned myself living in the US or even leaving Romania, but seeing the opportunities I was missing, just for not being in the US, encouraged me to take the wild leap and follow this dream.

My three-year immigration process is a story for another day, but I'm very grateful to be here and to have so many opportunities nonexistent in my small Romanian home-town. I've been in the US for almost two years as I'm writing this and I'm still utterly fascinated by America. My mind is blown every time I walk into an American grocery store. If you've been living here your whole life, you might be wondering, "What's so fascinating about it?" Let's just start with the chip aisle, an aisle I always have to make a stop in, no matter if I need a bag of chips or not. As someone who had access to maybe four different potato chip flavors growing up—salt, cheese, paprika, sour cream and onion—seeing one hundred different flavors from dill pickle, to mustard, to birthday cake will never not be mind-blowing. I'm also not over the convenience of buying a bag of plain white marshmallows, without having to make them from scratch, or being able to find a bag of cranberries at all times, without having to visit ten differ-ent stores and call four people in order to get to it.

Funny enough, in the same way I was missing canned pumpkin puree or cran-berry sauce in Romania, I am now missing things like fresh bread, roadside wine, or juicy summer tomatoes from my favorite farmers' market in my hometown. Living this experience is beautiful, and it makes me appreciate the small things in each stage of my life!

I also can't believe I'm writing my first cookbook. It feels like a dream—one I never dared to dream—that came true. I'm so grateful to everyone who believed in me and helped me get to where I am.

At this moment, I have almost two million people in my online community, millions of recipe views, and hundreds of millions of views of my food videos. And yet, I still remember the first time someone re-created one of my recipes. It didn't feel real at all. I didn't think anyone was actually going to read my recipes, let alone re-create them. I jumped on my phone and double-checked the recipe to ensure everything was fine. You'd think that excitement would fizzle out the more people make your recipes. The opposite of that happens: It gets more and more exciting with every single recipe.

I can't explain the joy and thrill I feel putting it all in a book for you, one that will live on your counter and is there for you for every occasion. I am so grateful for this journey and that I get to share my passion and love of food with you in this cookbook. I hope you're inspired to bring joy to your loved ones when you make my recipes in your own home.

get prepped

This page will make your cooking less stressful and your food significantly better. Read it!

You Know Best

I always encourage cooks to loosely follow the time estimates in the recipes, and focus on the visual. If a recipe calls for sautéing a shallot until translucent and soft, about 4 minutes, but your shallot doesn't look like that after 4 minutes, give it more time. The same goes if the shallot starts burning after 2 minutes. Reduce the heat or set the pan aside. There are so many variables related to the estimated cooking time, from the type of stove you're using, the material of your pan, to the altitude you're cooking at. The same goes for the oven: If something is cooking, keep an eye on it! Some ovens get hotter, some stay cold, some have a stronger top burner, some are electric, some work on gas. You know your oven best, so trust your intuition.

Make It Your Own

I often get asked permission to swap ingredients in nonbaking recipes. You don't need my permission, just go for it! It's how you learn your way in the kitchen. Do you absolutely hate cilantro? Use parsley instead. Not a fan of cottage cheese? You might enjoy ricotta. Not a cumin person? Try a different warm spice or simply omit it.

Salt It All

Knowing how to season food is one of the most crucial skills to develop in the kitchen. I purposely left most salt measurements up to you. I like my food salty, but if you want to lower your sodium intake, season your food accordingly. Taste and season as you go—especially soups and stews, those will always need extra pinches of salt. I encourage you to get your hands on a pack of flaky salt—it's perfect for finishing your dishes and adding texture to each bite.

All recipes in this book use Diamond Crystal kosher salt. If using other salt brands, make sure to adjust the salt measurement accordingly.

Oily Business

If I had to pick an oil to cook with for the rest of my life, I would confidently choose extra-virgin olive oil. It's simply perfect, love it, 10/10 (iykyk!). It has an amazing flavor, it's versatile and significantly better for you compared to other oils—you'll always find it in my pantry.

When it comes to neutral oil—a flavorless oil that wouldn't alter the taste of a dish—I like using grapeseed oil, sunflower seed oil, or avocado oil (this one's bougie), especially when a significant amount ends up in a dish: For example, if I'm baking a cake or whipping up a dressing that calls for neutral oil, I'd use one of the previously mentioned oils, but if I need to deep-fry food in cups and cups of oil, I'd go for something more affordable like canola, peanut, or vegetable oil.

Pasta PSA

Some will encourage you to keep your pasta water as salty as the ocean—I'm not a fan of that. Since pasta water plays such an important role in the sauce, too much salt will be overwhelming. Pasta water should be salty enough for you to be able to season food with or sip on it. Two or three big pinches of kosher salt in a large pot of water are plenty.

Flour Talks

When baking using cup measurements, give your flour a quick, dry whisk in its container before scooping it into the measuring cup and leveling it out with a knife. This additional step will ensure a more consistent result throughout your baking. My cup of flour weighs 125 grams after measuring this way, every single time.

Let's Get Citrusy!

Some recipes in this book use whole Meyer lemons. Suppose you can't find any, since they're not as widely available. In that case, other lemons (or other citrus for that matter) *should* do the job, but here are a few characteristics you should have in mind when picking a lemon (or any citrus): Make sure the fruit has a thin, smooth skin; it shouldn't be thick and super porous. Gently squeeze the fruit: You should be able to easily squeeze it in your palm. If it's hard to squeeze, pick a different one. The thinner the skin, the juicier the citrus and the less pith (therefore less bitterness) you'll have to deal with.

egg-stravaganza

Sesame-Crusted Breakfast Quesadilla
with Spinach

Serves 2 | Prep Time: 10 minutes | Cook Time: 15 minutes | Total Time: 25 minutes

A cheesy egg quesadilla is one of my most commonly made breakfasts, since tortillas and eggs are a staple in my fridge. This sesame-crusted version is what I make when I want to zhuzh up this breakfast favorite of mine. I like to describe it as the perfect cross between a sesame bagel egg sandwich and a quesadilla. I love making this recipe for my guests as it's so easy to double, triple, or quadruple the quantities. It comes together so easily and it's truly a joy seeing their reaction: You get the crunchy first bite, the creamy cheese pull, the silky custardy eggs and tender spinach—talk about a texture paradise.

2 large eggs

2 (7-inch) flour tortillas

2 tablespoons sesame seeds

⅓ cup cottage cheese

Kosher salt

1 tablespoon neutral oil, such as sunflower or grapeseed

2 cups packed baby spinach

2 garlic cloves, thinly sliced

¼ teaspoon Aleppo pepper or red chile flakes

½ cup coarsely grated low-moisture mozzarella or cheddar cheese (about 2 ounces)

Hot sauce or salsa, for serving

In a medium bowl, whisk the eggs until fully combined. Using a pastry brush or your fingers, lightly brush one side of each tortilla with egg. Evenly sprinkle 1 tablespoon sesame seeds on the egg-brushed side of each tortilla.

Add the cottage cheese and a pinch of salt to the bowl of eggs and stir to combine.

In an 8-inch nonstick skillet (see Note), heat the oil over medium heat. Add the spinach and a pinch of salt and cook, stirring, until the spinach is wilted, 3 to 4 minutes. Add the garlic and Aleppo pepper and cook until fragrant, about 1 minute. Add the egg mixture to the pan, using a silicone spatula to evenly distribute the spinach throughout the eggs. Cook until the edges begin to set but the center is still raw and jiggly, 1 to 2 minutes.

Place one of the tortillas on top of the eggs, sesame-side up. Cook until the eggs have set and are sticking to the tortilla, 3 to 4 minutes. Use a spatula to flip the whole stack egg-side up. (You can also use a plate for this maneuver: Remove the pan from the heat and invert a 9-inch [or larger] plate on top of the pan. Carefully, with your palm on the plate, flip the pan over so the eggs and tortilla land on the plate, tortilla-side down. Slide the stack back into the pan and return it to the heat.)

Top the egg with the grated cheese and the remaining tortilla, sesame-side up. Cover and cook until the sesame seeds on the underside are golden and the cheese is fully melted, 2 to 3 minutes. Flip the quesadilla again and cook to toast the sesame coating on the other tortilla, 1 to 2 minutes.

Cut into quarters and serve right away with hot sauce or salsa.

Note: *A nonstick skillet is key to preventing the sesame seeds from getting stuck on the bottom of the pan.*

Crispy Ketchup Rice
with Fried Eggs

Serves 1 or 2 | Prep Time: 5 minutes | Cook Time: 15 minutes | Total Time: 20 minutes

Chances are you have a ketchup bottle staring at you every time you open the fridge. To keep my ketchup from going to waste, I developed a recipe that makes me excited to use it up: a crispy, crunchy ketchup rice topped with perfectly fried eggs.

Ketchup, eggs, and rice aren't a new combo; a popular Japanese dish called omurice combines ketchup and an egg omelet atop fried rice. What's different with mine is how the crispy ketchup rice is seared like a patty: The sugary ketchup crisps up and caramelizes in the pan, creating a satisfying, tahdig-like, super-crunchy exterior. Then it's topped with a silky, runny egg yolk that floods into all the crunchy nooks and crannies.

1 cup day-old cooked white rice

¼ cup ketchup

½ teaspoon garlic powder

Dash of hot sauce (optional)

Kosher salt

3 tablespoons unsalted butter

1 or 2 large eggs

Finely chopped fresh dill, cilantro, or parsley, for serving

Flaky salt and freshly ground black pepper

In a medium bowl, stir together the cooked rice, ketchup, garlic powder, hot sauce (if using), and a pinch of kosher salt.

In an 8-inch nonstick pan, heat 1 tablespoon of the butter over medium heat until sizzling, about 2 minutes. Add the ketchup-rice mixture, pressing it down using a spatula to form a disc. Cook, undisturbed, until the underside is seared and crisp with dark red bits from the ketchup, 2 to 3 minutes. Peek underneath to make sure the rice isn't burning. Cook for 2 to 4 more minutes, as needed to get a crispy bottom.

Reduce the heat to medium-low. Using a spatula, carefully flip the rice cake (it's okay if it crumbles a bit, you can press the pieces back together after you flip). Slide another 1 tablespoon butter into the pan. Cook until the bottom is crispy and browned, 3 to 4 more minutes. Slide the rice onto a plate.

Return the pan to medium heat. Heat the remaining 1 tablespoon butter until sizzling. Add the eggs and season with kosher salt. Fry until the egg whites start setting while the area around the yolk is still translucent, another minute. Add 1 tablespoon water to the side of the pan. Cover with a lid and steam until the egg whites are fully cooked but the yolk is still a little wobbly, about 2 minutes. (Cook them longer if you'd like a more set yolk.)

Slide the eggs on top of the crispy rice, scatter the herbs on top, sprinkle with flaky salt and black pepper and serve.

Leek and Spinach Frittata
with Creamy Ricotta and Pesto

Serves 2 to 4 | Prep Time: 20 minutes | Cook Time: 40 minutes | Total Time: 1 hour

This leek-packed frittata embodies the essence of spring with its vibrant, herbaceous flavor, and makes a perfect breakfast meal, especially for feeding a crowd. It's rich with creamy cheese, and topped with a rustic coarse pesto. The best part is how much you can prep in advance. You can slice the leeks and keep them in cold water in the fridge, chop the garlic, and make the pesto ahead of time.

BONUS: any leftovers transform into fantastic breakfast sandwiches! Place a frittata wedge inside a split soft bun, add cheese, and grill until melty and toasty.

Pesto

1 cup packed fresh basil leaves

¼ cup freshly grated Parmesan cheese

2 tablespoons chopped fresh oregano (optional)

2 tablespoons any seeds or chopped nuts (pumpkin seeds or walnuts are great)

1 garlic clove, peeled

¼ cup extra-virgin olive oil

Kosher salt

Frittata

6 large eggs

Kosher salt

3 tablespoons extra-virgin olive oil

1 large leek, halved lengthwise, thoroughly cleaned, and thinly sliced (2 to 2½ cups)

1 cup packed baby spinach

2 garlic cloves, thinly sliced

7 ounces (¾ cup) whole-milk ricotta cheese

For Serving

A few small basil leaves, for garnish

Flaky salt and freshly ground black pepper

Crusty bread

Make the pesto: In a food processor, combine the basil, Parmesan, oregano (if using), seeds or nuts, and garlic and pulse a few times to break everything down a bit. Add the oil and a pinch of salt and continue pulsing until combined, aiming for a coarser texture.

Make the frittata: Preheat the oven to 400°F.

In a medium bowl, vigorously whisk the eggs and a good pinch of salt until fully combined, with no white streaks.

In an 8-inch ovenproof nonstick or well-seasoned cast-iron skillet, heat 2 tablespoons of the oil over medium heat. Add the leek and a pinch of salt and cook, stirring frequently, until the leeks are quite soft and have reduced in volume, 10 to 12 minutes. Add the spinach and cook, tossing with the leeks as you stir, until wilted, about 2 minutes. Add the garlic and cook until just fragrant, about 1 minute. Taste and adjust the seasoning. Remove the pan from the heat.

Add the leek mixture to the eggs and mix to coat the vegetables. Return the pan to medium heat and add the remaining 1 tablespoon oil, swirling it around the pan to coat evenly. Carefully add the egg mixture to the pan and cook until the egg starts to firm up around the edges and pull away from the pan, 5 to 6 minutes. Top with dollops of the ricotta.

Bake until the frittata looks firm on top, with no jiggles if you nudge the pan, 10 to 15 minutes.

To serve: Top with dollops of the pesto and the small basil leaves. Sprinkle flaky salt and black pepper over the frittata. Serve sliced into wedges, with crusty bread on the side.

Golden Baked Potato Cake
with Smoked Salmon and Poached Eggs

Serves 2 to 4 | Prep Time: 25 minutes | Cook Time: 35 minutes | Total Time: 1 hour

Imagine your favorite hash brown, then picture a bigger, crispier pan-fried potato cake. That, my friends, is a rösti. It's the unofficial national dish of Switzerland and my inspiration for this breakfast recipe. Unlike a traditional rösti, my potato cake is thicker, more compact, and partially baked to ensure a buttery tender center. It's packed with fennel seeds, black pepper, and fresh dill, subtle enough to not overpower the potato, but instead, complement it. But we don't stop there: As soon as the dilly potato cake comes out of the oven it's topped with cool, tangy crème fraîche, ribbons of smoked salmon, and soft poached eggs.

Potato Cake and Poached Eggs

½ teaspoon fennel seeds

½ teaspoon black peppercorns

1½ pounds Yukon Gold potatoes (4 or 5 medium)

¼ cup chopped fresh dill

8 tablespoons (4 ounces) unsalted butter, cubed

Kosher salt

2 to 4 large eggs

For Serving

¼ to ½ cup crème fraîche or sour cream

2 to 4 ounces smoked salmon

Torn fresh dill

Lemon zest (optional)

Flaky salt and freshly ground black pepper

Prepared or freshly grated horseradish (optional)

Make the potato cake: Preheat the oven to 425°F.

Add the fennel seeds and peppercorns to a mortar and pestle. Crush roughly, just enough to break them open but not grind into a powder. (You can also do this by putting the spices in a bag or between paper kitchen towels and crushing roughly with a rolling pin.)

Scrub and rinse the potatoes thoroughly. (No need to peel them.) Fill a medium bowl with cold water. Use the coarse side of a box grater to shred the potatoes, holding them lengthwise to get longer potato shreds—they're more likely to stick together and give the potato cake a better structure. Swish the potato shreds around in the cold water and drain.

Place the potatoes on a clean kitchen towel, gather up the corners of the towel, twist, and squeeze out as much liquid as possible. Retwist and squeeze again until no more water drips out. Return the potatoes to the empty bowl and add the dill.

In an 8-inch well-seasoned cast-iron or ovenproof nonstick skillet, combine the butter and crushed fennel seeds and peppercorns. Cook over medium heat, stirring, until the butter is melted and the spices are fragrant, 2 to 3 minutes. Remove the pan from the heat.

Pour the spiced butter over the grated potatoes and season with a big pinch of salt. Toss well to coat the potatoes and dill in butter.

Return the skillet to medium heat and add the potato mixture. Using a spatula, press it down to pack it in the skillet. Cook, undisturbed, until the edges of the potato cake start pulling away from the pan and turn translucent, 4 to 7 minutes.

Transfer the skillet to the oven and bake until golden, 25 to 28 minutes. Preheat the broiler. Place the oven rack about 4 inches from the heating element. Broil the potato cake until crisp, about 2 minutes.

(recipe continues)

Poach the eggs: Rest a fine-mesh strainer over a bowl. Crack each egg over the fine-mesh strainer to drain off any watery bits that can result in a stringy poached egg. Add the cracked eggs to another bowl, making sure the yolks stay intact.

Bring a medium pot of water to a boil. Reduce the heat to low for a gentle simmer. Using a spoon, stir the water in a circle a few times to create a little vortex. Slowly lower the eggs in the vortex. Simmer until the egg whites are opaque and fully cooked, 1½ to 2 minutes. Using a slotted spoon, gently lift out the eggs and pat the yolk with your finger: For a runny yolk, the yolk should feel wobbly and the egg white firm and bouncy. Transfer the eggs to a plate.

To serve: Place a large plate over the skillet with the potato cake. Carefully flip the skillet to set the potato cake on the plate. Dollop the crème fraîche or sour cream on top, followed by a few ribbons of the smoked salmon. Top with poached eggs, dill, lemon zest (if using), flaky salt, lots of black pepper, and horseradish (if using).

One-Pan Zucchini Feta Fried Eggs

Serves 2 | Prep Time: 5 minutes | Cook Time: 15 minutes | Total Time: 20 minutes

A huge chunk of my time in the kitchen is spent figuring out how to use the zucchini I have that are about to go bad. I woke up one morning with three almost-floppy zucchini waiting for me to notice them, and that's how this simple, scrappy zucchini dish with melty feta was born. It became my breakfast and lunch fixation for the rest of the month. While most of my recipe fixations end with my not wanting to see them ever again, this one had a different ending. To this day, it remains one of my favorite dishes to make at the peak of zucchini season.

3 tablespoons extra-virgin olive oil

1 pound zucchini (about 2 medium), cut into ½-inch coins

Kosher salt and freshly ground black pepper

4 large eggs

⅓ cup crumbled feta cheese (about 1.5 ounces)

Finely grated lemon zest, for garnish

Aleppo pepper or red chile flakes, for serving

Chopped fresh dill and parsley, for serving

Warm bread, such as baguette, sourdough bread, or No-Fuss Focaccia (page 65)

In a 10- to 12-inch well-seasoned cast-iron skillet, heat the olive oil over medium heat until nearly smoking, about 2 minutes. Arrange the zucchini slices in the skillet in a mostly even layer (a little overlap is okay). Season with salt and black pepper and cook, undisturbed, until the zucchini is golden and slightly crispy underneath, 3 to 4 minutes. Flip the zucchini and cook until golden and crispy all over, 3 to 4 more minutes.

In the middle of the skillet, make a couple of spaces between the zucchini for the eggs. Crack the eggs into the little wells, season with salt and black pepper, and cook until the whites begin to set, 2 to 3 minutes.

Sprinkle the crumbled feta all over the mixture and cover with a lid. The moisture from the zucchini will steam the eggs gently. Cook until the egg whites are fully cooked and opaque but the yolk is still wobbly to the touch, 2 to 4 minutes. Remove the pan from the heat.

Top with lemon zest, a sprinkle of Aleppo or chile flakes, and the fresh herbs. Serve with bread on the side.

Turkish Eggs
with Spiced Butter and Garlicky Yogurt

Serves 2 | Prep Time: 10 minutes | Cook Time: 5 minutes | Total Time: 15 minutes

This dish, also known as çılbır, is a garlicky bowl of yogurt topped with soft poached eggs and a sizzling hot, spiced butter. It's fragrant, luscious, and so easy to make. It will surely be a recipe you'll keep coming back to. Make sure you've got some bread on hand. Cool, thick yogurt swirled with the hot, spiced egg is a magical way to start your day.

Garlicky Yogurt

2½ cups whole-milk Greek yogurt (see Note)

2 garlic cloves, finely grated or minced

3 tablespoons finely chopped fresh dill

2 tablespoons fresh lemon juice

Kosher salt

Turkish Eggs

4 tablespoons (2 ounces) unsalted butter

1 teaspoon Aleppo pepper or red chile flakes

½ teaspoon cumin seeds

2 to 4 large eggs

Kosher salt

For Serving

Chopped fresh dill

Flaky salt

Lemon wedges

Fresh pita or crusty bread

Make the garlicky yogurt: In a medium bowl, whisk together the yogurt, garlic, dill, lemon juice, and a pinch of kosher salt. Divide the yogurt mixture between two shallow serving bowls.

Make the Turkish eggs: In a small saucepan, heat the butter over medium heat until sizzling, 2 to 3 minutes. Remove the pan from the heat. Stir in the Aleppo pepper and cumin seeds. Set aside for later.

Crack each egg over a fine-mesh strainer to drain off any watery bits that can result in a stringy poached egg. Add the eggs to a small heatproof bowl.

Bring a small saucepan of well-salted water to a boil over medium-high heat. Reduce the heat to a gentle simmer, medium-low to low. Using a spoon or spatula, stir the simmering water in a circle a few times to create a little vortex. Slowly add the eggs in the vortex and simmer until the egg whites are opaque and fully cooked, 1½ to 2 minutes. Using a slotted spoon, gently lift out the eggs and pat the yolk with your finger: For a runny yolk, the yolk should feel wobbly and the egg white firm and bouncy. Transfer the eggs to the serving bowls, and set right on top of the yogurt.

To serve: Drizzle the warm spiced butter all over the eggs and top with more dill and flaky salt. Serve with lemon wedges and pita or bread.

Note: *While this dish is traditionally made with Turkish yogurt, Greek yogurt and other thick strained yogurts will also work. If you can find Turkish yogurt at a local market, definitely give it a go!*

Blistered Tomato Toast
with Jammy Egg

Serves 1 | Prep Time: 5 minutes | Cook Time: 10 minutes | Total Time: 15 minutes

Tell me the thought of this doesn't get you drooling: sweet, charred tomatoes bursting with every bite, creamy yolk flooding the toast, the contrast between the hot tomatoes and the cold cheese, and the satisfying crunch of crusty, garlicky bread. This breakfast is a full-on experience from start to finish.

　　NOW LET'S TALK COTTAGE CHEESE. I love the texture, especially of the large-curd variety, and I enjoy its richness and mild dairy taste. That said, I know there are cottage cheese haters out there! There are still lots of ways to love this dish: Simply swap out the cottage cheese for creamy ricotta, tangy labneh, or Greek yogurt.

1 large egg

1 cup cherry tomatoes

1 tablespoon extra-virgin olive oil, plus more for drizzling

Kosher salt

1 thick slice sourdough bread or any other crusty bread

1 garlic clove (optional)

⅓ cup cottage cheese, ricotta cheese, or Greek yogurt

Freshly ground black pepper

2 tablespoons chopped fresh dill or parsley

Flaky salt, for serving

Bring a small saucepan of water to a boil over medium-high heat. Gently lower the egg into the boiling water and cook for 6 to 7 minutes for a jammy egg, or closer to 9 minutes for a more set yolk. Place the egg in a bowl of cold water to cool.

Heat a medium cast-iron skillet over medium heat until gently smoking, about 4 minutes. Add the tomatoes and olive oil and let the tomatoes sear, undisturbed, until slightly charred underneath, 2 to 3 minutes. Carefully shake the skillet back and forth to move the tomatoes in the pan. Cook until the tomatoes are blistered and some have burst, about 2 more minutes. Remove the pan from the heat. Season with a pinch of kosher salt.

Toast the bread to your preference. If using, rub the garlic clove all over the toasted bread.

Set the toast on a plate and dollop on the cottage cheese. Sprinkle with a pinch of kosher salt and a few grinds of black pepper. Top with the blistered tomatoes and any juices from the pan, followed by the herbs. Peel the egg and set it on top. Slice the egg in half to let the yolk run down the toast, and finish with a drizzle of olive oil, flaky salt, and more black pepper.

Breakfast Tacos
with Crispy Spiced Chickpeas and Spicy Scallion Salsa

Serves 4 | Prep Time: 20 minutes | Cook Time: 25 minutes | Total Time: 45 minutes

Don't let the name fool you: Just because these tacos are stuffed with scrambled eggs doesn't mean you can eat them only for breakfast. They make a perfectly hearty lunch or a quick and easy dinner, packed with lots of filling protein. You've got scrambled cottage cheese eggs, crispy spiced chickpeas (you won't get enough of these!), and an extra dollop of cottage cheese on each taco. The brightness of the zesty scallion salsa brings all the flavors together and will have you going in for seconds (and thirds).

Spiced Chickpeas

1 (15-ounce) can chickpeas, drained and rinsed

3 tablespoons extra-virgin olive oil

½ teaspoon sweet paprika

½ teaspoon cumin seeds

Kosher salt

Scallion Salsa

2 scallions, thinly sliced

1 jalapeño, thinly sliced

¼ cup finely chopped fresh cilantro

2 tablespoons extra-virgin olive oil

Grated zest and juice of 1 lime

Kosher salt

Cottage Cheese Scrambled Eggs

4 large eggs

½ cup cottage cheese (see Note)

2 tablespoons unsalted butter

Kosher salt

Assembly

8 small (street taco size) corn tortillas

Cottage cheese

Hot sauce

Make the spiced chickpeas: Preheat the oven to 425°F.

Add the chickpeas to a baking sheet and roll a kitchen or paper towel over them to remove excess moisture. Add the olive oil, paprika, cumin seeds, and a pinch of salt and toss to coat.

Roast until crispy, about 20 minutes, nudging the pan halfway through to move the chickpeas around. Set aside to cool.

Make the scallion salsa: In a medium bowl, combine the scallions, jalapeño, cilantro, olive oil, lime zest, lime juice, and a pinch of salt. Toss to combine.

Make the cottage cheese scrambled eggs: In a medium bowl, combine the eggs and cottage cheese, whisking vigorously.

In a medium nonstick skillet, melt the butter over medium heat and heat until sizzling, 2 to 3 minutes. Add the egg mixture and use a silicone spatula to go around the edges of the pan, pushing the cooked eggs toward the center of the pan. Season with a pinch of salt. Tilt the pan to let the uncooked egg mixture run back around the pan, and repeat until the eggs are mostly cooked but a bit custardy, about 4 minutes. Remove the pan from the heat and cover.

Assemble the tacos: Preheat the broiler. Place the oven rack about 4 inches from the heating element.

Arrange the tortillas in a single layer on a baking sheet, letting them overlap here and there if necessary. Broil until the tortillas are warm and slightly charred, 3 to 4 minutes. You could also warm up the tortillas in a dry skillet, on the stove.

Top each tortilla with a spoonful of custardy eggs, some cottage cheese, scallion salsa, and the crispy spiced chickpeas. Drizzle with hot sauce all over and serve right away.

Note: *I've got some alternatives for those who aren't cottage cheese fans or willing to make the leap for now. Swap it out for Greek yogurt or ricotta to achieve similar results.*

Dutch Baby Pancake
with Yogurt Whipped Cream and Sweet Berries

Serves 2 to 4 | Prep Time: 20 minutes | Cook Time: 20 minutes | Total Time: 40 minutes

Featuring a giant sweet pancake in my egg chapter might seem a stretch, but this tender Dutch baby relies on lots of eggs for its impressive lift. It combines the light, airy feel of a popover with the sweetness of a pancake. No matter how many times I've made this, I still can't get my eyes off it while it's baking. The pancake puffs up like a sassy soufflé in the oven. Then the crunchy sugar-coated center collapses, setting the perfect stage for the star: a tangy whipped cream topped with sweet, juicy berries.

Macerated Berries and Yogurt Whipped Cream

1 cup (5 oz/150g) berries, such as raspberries, chopped strawberries, or blueberries

1 tablespoon (13g) granulated sugar

½ cup (123g) heavy cream

½ cup (123g) whole-milk Greek yogurt

2 tablespoons (14g) powdered sugar

Dutch Baby Pancake

4 large eggs

¼ cup (50g) plus 1 tablespoon (13g) granulated sugar

½ cup (123g) whole milk

2 teaspoons (9g) vanilla extract

½ teaspoon (3g) kosher salt

⅔ cup (85g) all-purpose flour

3 tablespoons (45g) unsalted butter

For Serving

Powdered sugar, for dusting

Fresh mint leaves, for garnish

Make the macerated berries and yogurt whipped cream: In a medium bowl, mix together the berries and granulated sugar. Set aside to macerate.

In a medium bowl, with a hand mixer or whisk, whip the cream to soft peaks. Add the yogurt and powdered sugar and continue whipping to stiff peaks. Refrigerate the yogurt whipped cream until you're ready to serve.

Make the Dutch baby pancake: Place an oven rack in the center of the oven. Preheat the oven to 425°F.

In a medium bowl, combine the eggs and ¼ cup (50g) of the granulated sugar and whisk vigorously until smooth and pale yellow. Add the milk, vanilla, and salt and whisk until combined. Add the flour and vigorously whisk until the batter is totally smooth. (You can also make this in a blender to ensure a super-smooth batter.)

In an 8- to 10-inch ovenproof cast-iron or stainless steel skillet, melt the butter over medium heat. Let it heat until it's sizzling and a bit foamy on top, 3 to 4 minutes. Quickly and carefully add the batter and evenly sprinkle the remaining 1 tablespoon granulated sugar on top.

Transfer the skillet to the oven and bake until the pancake is puffy but firm to the touch, golden brown on the edges, and golden yellow in the center, 17 to 20 minutes. The pancake will start to deflate as soon as it comes out of the oven, so plan to serve it right away if you can. (If you can't, that's okay too—it'll taste just as good!)

To serve: Dust the Dutch baby with powdered sugar and top with the yogurt whipped cream and macerated berries. Garnish with mint leaves, slice, and serve warm.

Herby Egg Salad
with Lemon and Capers

Serves 2 to 4 | Prep Time: 20 minutes, plus 30 minutes chilling | Cook Time: 10 minutes | Total Time: 1 hour

For me, a classic egg salad sandwich has it all: creamy, salty, eggy, and soft. This riffs on the classic egg-and-mayo pairing, but adds some briny, zesty elements to balance out the richness. The lemon zest, lemon juice, and briny capers bring the perfect level of acidity to brighten things up, the scallions and herbs bring zingy green freshness, and the horseradish gives everything that secret sharp kick. If we were eating this in my kitchen, I'd choose a crusty, toasted rye as the base for the egg salad, but a soft white bread would be a close second.

6 large eggs

¼ cup mayonnaise

2 scallions, finely chopped

2 tablespoons finely chopped
    fresh parsley or dill

1 tablespoon brined capers,
    drained, rinsed, and chopped

1 tablespoon whole-grain mustard
    (optional)

Grated zest and juice of ½ lemon

1 teaspoon freshly grated or
    prepared horseradish (optional)

Kosher salt and freshly ground
    black pepper

Lightly toasted or fried bread, for
    serving

Fill a medium bowl with ice and water.

Bring a medium pot of water to a boil. Carefully add the eggs to the pot and boil for 10 minutes. Using a slotted spoon, transfer the boiled eggs to the ice bath and chill for 30 minutes or until completely cool (no warm eggs in the egg salad!).

In a medium bowl, stir together the mayonnaise, scallions, parsley, capers, mustard (if using), lemon zest, lemon juice, horseradish (if using), a big pinch of salt, and several grinds of pepper.

Peel and roughly chop the boiled eggs. Add them to the bowl with the dressing and fold to combine. Taste and adjust the seasoning with more salt or lemon juice as needed.

Serve on a slice of toasted or fried bread, or turn it into a sandwich.

nosh & nibble

Rosemary Olive Shortbread

Makes about 24 shortbreads | Prep Time: 30 minutes, plus 30 minutes chilling | Cook Time: 35 minutes | Total Time: 1 hour 35 minutes

Developing this recipe has been so relaxing. You should make these for the smell that permeates your kitchen and house; they're scent-sational! It's better than any fancy candle you could light up in your kitchen. From the olive oil–fried olives to the oil infused with rosemary and garlic, the mix of smells couldn't get more inviting than this. The final result has a beautifully golden crust that snaps, then immediately melts in your mouth, releasing all the delicious umami flavors you've smelled while making them.

1 cup (130g) pitted kalamata olives (see Note), drained and finely chopped

¼ cup (55g) extra-virgin olive oil

4 garlic cloves, finely chopped

2 fresh rosemary sprigs, leaves finely chopped

2 cups (250g) all-purpose flour

2 teaspoons (6g) garlic powder

1½ teaspoons (4g) kosher salt

8 tablespoons (4 oz/113g) unsalted butter, at room temperature

5 ounces (140g) sharp aged cheese, such as Gruyère, Parmesan, or sharp cheddar, finely grated

1 large egg yolk

1 tablespoon (13g) ice water

In a small saucepan, combine the olives and oil and cook over medium heat, stirring occasionally, until the olives turn a deep purple-brown color, about 15 minutes. (We're partially frying the olives to remove excess moisture.) Remove the pan from the heat. Stir in the garlic and rosemary.

In a medium bowl, whisk together the flour, garlic powder, and salt. Add the olive mixture and stir to combine, until the flour is clumpy, a bit like wet sand. Add the butter and use your hands to work it into the flour mixture. Mix in the cheese. Add the egg yolk and ice water and mix until the dough holds together when pressed.

Line a work surface with a sheet of plastic wrap. Dump the dough onto the plastic wrap. Using your hands, roughly shape it into an 8-inch log. Gently press down on the log until it's about 1½ inches high, 9½ inches long, and 3 to 3½ inches wide. Tightly wrap the dough in the plastic wrap and freeze for at least 30 minutes.

Preheat the oven to 350°F. Line two baking sheets with parchment paper.

Unwrap the cold dough. You'll want to move fast to keep the shortbreads cold. Using a knife or bench scraper, slice the log into 24 slices (a touch thinner than ½ inch thick). Arrange the shortbreads on the baking sheets, leaving about ½ inch between them—they'll puff slightly in the oven but won't spread much. If you can't fit both sheets in the oven at the same time, store the remaining one in the fridge.

Bake until crisp and golden, 28 to 35 minutes.

Cool completely on the pan, then serve right away or store in an airtight container at room temperature.

Note: *For those who are intrigued by the idea of a savory shortbread but are turned off by the presence of olives, chopped sun-dried tomatoes (the same amount, fried the same way) would be incredible: a little sweet, tart, and lending a beautifully rich color to the dough.*

Spicy Charred Red Pepper Yogurt Dip

Serves 4 to 6 | Prep Time: 20 minutes | Cook Time: 10 minutes | Total Time: 30 minutes

There's nothing like a rich meze spread packed with simple dips and fresh bread when guests come over! I can't get enough of this one: It's roasted, spicy, smoky red peppers dolloped over a bed of thick Greek yogurt. The yogurt is a must; its cool temperature and refreshing tang are the perfect balance to the spicy salsa. The heat comes from using red jalapeños in the mix, and you can adjust the heat level with how many you use, and whether you remove the seeds or leave them in.

Spicy Charred Red Peppers

2 medium red bell peppers, halved and seeded

2 red jalapeños or Fresno chiles, halved

⅓ cup extra-virgin olive oil, plus more as needed

3 tablespoons rice vinegar

3 tablespoons finely chopped fresh cilantro or parsley

3 garlic cloves, minced or finely grated

½ teaspoon Aleppo pepper or red chile flakes

Kosher salt

Yogurt

3 cups whole-milk Greek yogurt

1 garlic clove, minced or finely grated

Kosher salt and freshly ground black pepper

Chips, crackers, or crusty bread, for serving

Make the spicy charred red peppers: Place an oven rack about 4 inches under the top heating element. Preheat the oven to 450°F.

Arrange the peppers and chiles on a baking sheet, cut-sides down. Roast the peppers, checking on them frequently, until charred and blistered all over, 8 to 10 minutes.

Using tongs, transfer the peppers and chiles to a medium bowl. Cover with a plate or a lid to trap in steam for 10 minutes. They will steam in the bowl, making them easier to peel. Peel them by pinching the skin with your fingers, slipping the charred skin right off. (If some uncharred skin doesn't want to come off, that's okay!)

Finely chop the peppers and chiles and return them to the bowl. Add the oil, vinegar, cilantro, garlic, Aleppo pepper, and a pinch of salt and stir to combine. Taste and adjust the seasoning as needed.

Prepare the yogurt: In a medium bowl, combine the yogurt, garlic, a hefty pinch of salt, and several grinds of black pepper.

Swirl the yogurt on a serving platter, creating a well in the middle. Pile the red pepper salsa in the well, drizzling any juices around the yogurt. Serve with chips, crackers, or crusty bread.

Note: *If you're left with any scrappy bits of the spicy dip at the bottom of the serving bowl, don't throw them away! Save them in the fridge for the next day and spoon on top of a soft-boiled egg and a dollop of cottage cheese for an easy breakfast.*

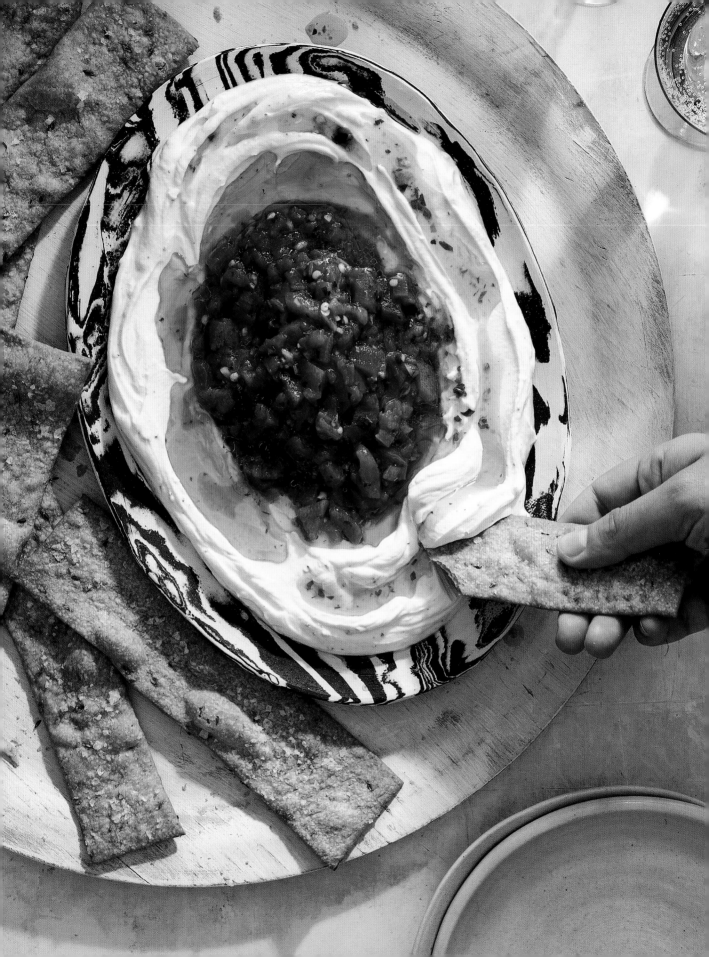

Gruyère-Stuffed Dates
with Salted Sesame Honey

Serves 4 to 6 | Prep Time: 7 minutes | Cook Time: 3 minutes | Total Time: 10 minutes

I believe I have the ideal ten-minute, sweet, snacky appetizer that's perfect for when you have last-minute guests. I'm talking about jammy, sesame honey–drizzled Gruyère-stuffed dates. We've got nutty, sharp chunks of Gruyère packed inside caramel-y, toffee-like dates and topped with a crunchy honey sesame sauce—it's truly an incredible bite. I know it might not seem like a lot, but this bite-size app is so rich and filling that you won't need many to feel full.

2 ounces Gruyère cheese

6 Medjool dates, pitted and halved

3 tablespoons sesame seeds

3 tablespoons honey

Flaky salt

Place the Gruyère on a small cutting board. Using the tip of a paring knife, break off 12 craggy bite-size chunks of cheese. Place a piece of cheese in each date half, pressing down gently to make the cheese stick.

In a small skillet, toast the sesame seeds over medium heat, shaking the pan frequently to keep them from burning, until just golden and fragrant, 2 to 3 minutes. Remove the pan from the heat. Add the honey to the skillet and stir to combine.

Drizzle the sesame honey over the stuffed dates and sprinkle flaky salt on top and serve.

Note: *These dates are also great warm, so don't hesitate making them in advance and allowing them to come to room temperature naturally. Or pop them in the microwave or oven for 15 seconds or so. You're not looking to melt the cheese, just warm it up a bit.*

Cumin-Spiced Long Snacking Crackers

Makes about 12 large crackers | Prep Time: 15 minutes | Cook Time: 25 minutes | Total Time: 40 minutes

Are homemade crackers worth it? I'd say yes, if they're not something you can buy at any store, like these snacking crackers—and you'll be surprised how easily they come together. These crackers are long and wide, and so fun to snap, dip, share, and eat. Spiced with cumin, they develop an inviting warmth and peppery, smoky sharpness. I like using both finely ground cumin and whole cumin seeds: The ground cumin flavors the dough while the whole seeds bring texture and pungency. To further enhance the spices, you'll bloom them in olive oil for maximal flavor.

These pair incredibly well with the Spicy Charred Red Pepper Yogurt Dip (page 50), Smoky Spiced Eggplant Dip (page 61), or Feta Dip (page 70), or just serve with a bit of cheese and grilled vegetables.

2 cups (250g) all-purpose flour, plus more for dusting

1 teaspoon (3g) kosher salt

½ teaspoon baking powder

¼ cup (53g) extra-virgin olive oil, plus more for brushing

1 tablespoon (10g) whole cumin seeds

1 tablespoon (8g) ground cumin

½ cup (113g) lukewarm water

Flaky salt, for topping

Preheat the oven to 400°F. Line one large or two standard baking sheets with parchment paper.

In a medium bowl, whisk together the flour, kosher salt, and baking powder.

In a small saucepan, combine the olive oil, cumin seeds, and ground cumin. Heat the oil and spices over medium-low heat, stirring frequently, until fragrant and toasty, 7 to 8 minutes. Remove the pan from the heat.

Add the spiced oil to the dry ingredients, scraping all the cumin seeds into the bowl. Mix using a silicone spatula or wooden spoon until combined. The mixture will be crumbly and dry. Add the water and mix until everything is combined and you're left with a smooth dough. Give it a quick knead if needed.

Place a large sheet of parchment paper on your work surface. Using your hands, shape the dough into a flat rectangle. Place the dough in the center of the parchment and lightly dust it with flour. Using a floured rolling pin, roll out the dough out as thinly as you can manage, keeping the rectangle shape as best you can. The rolled-out dough should roughly measure 12 × 16 inches and be ¹⁄₁₆ to ⅛ inch thick.

Using a pizza cutter or knife, trim the edges of the dough to form a clean rectangle. Reserve the scraps. Cut the dough in half crosswise and lengthwise, forming 4 smaller rectangles. Cut each rectangle lengthwise, into 3 long strips (about 2 × 8 inches). Arrange the strips of dough on the baking sheet, leaving about ½ inch between them. (If you run out of room, you can bake off a second batch, including the dough scraps.)

Add a few tablespoons of olive oil to a small bowl. Using a pastry brush, brush the tops of the crackers with oil. Top with flaky salt.

Bake until the crackers are puffed in certain spots, darker on the edges, and crisp to the touch, 12 to 15 minutes. Set aside to cool and repeat with any remaining dough.

Garlicky Tomato Ricotta Crostini

Serves 6 to 8 | Prep Time: 20 minutes | Cook Time: 10 minutes | Total Time: 30 minutes

Pan con tomate is a Spanish delight that shows us that the simplest ingredients can lead to the tastiest results. Grated, seasoned tomatoes, scooped over bread fried in olive oil, sometimes topped with a little anchovy fillet—I could eat pan con tomate all summer long.

Taking inspiration from that perfect bite, I decided to spin the classic and dollop the grated tomatoes over a cloud of whipped ricotta. The cheese is creamy, light, and mild in flavor, which makes it the perfect accompaniment to the tomatoes. It's an amazing, no-fuss appetizer.

3 medium tomatoes (about 1 pound)

2 garlic cloves, finely grated or minced

Kosher salt

1 cup whole-milk ricotta cheese

½ cup crème fraîche or sour cream

1 pound baguette or ciabatta

Extra-virgin olive oil, for drizzling

1 cup kalamata olives, pitted and halved

Flaky salt, for sprinkling

Preheat the oven to 425°F. Line a baking sheet with parchment paper.

Cut the tomatoes in half. Over a medium bowl, grate the tomatoes on the coarse holes of a box grater with the cut side of the tomatoes touching the blade. (You will be left with just the tomato skin, which I like to throw some salt on and snack on.) Add the garlic and a big pinch of kosher salt, and stir to combine.

In a food processor, process the ricotta until smooth, 1 to 2 minutes. Add the crème fraîche and a pinch of kosher salt and process until combined, another 20 to 30 seconds. Transfer the mixture to a bowl and refrigerate while you make the crostini.

Cut the bread into ½-inch-thick slices and place the slices on the baking sheet. Drizzle generously with olive oil. Bake until the bread is golden and crunchy on top, 6 to 8 minutes.

Using a fine-mesh strainer, drain off any excess liquid from the grated tomato mixture.

Spoon a small dollop of the whipped ricotta on each crostini and make a well in the middle with the back of the spoon. Add a spoonful of the grated tomatoes right in the middle, a halved olive on top, and a drizzle of olive oil. Lightly sprinkle flaky salt on top. Serve right away.

Note: *To make this ahead, prep the components up to 2 days in advance and assemble the crostini right before serving so the bread stays crisp.*

Butter Pecan Twists

Serves 4 to 6 | Prep Time: 25 minutes, plus 50 minutes chilling | Cook Time: 25 minutes |
Total Time: 1 hour 40 minutes

While most recipes in this chapter are savory, I wanted to offer you some sweet snacking alternatives. These rich, butter pecan twists are an amazing treat to display on your table, whether you're having someone over for breakfast or for cheese and wine. The butter pecan filling alone will be hard to resist when you make them, though if pecans don't speak to you, use another nut, such as almonds, walnuts, or pistachios. Dip these in coffee or tea for the ultimate morning treat.

2 cups (226g) pecans, finely chopped

4 tablespoons (2 oz/60g) unsalted butter

¾ cup packed (150g) dark brown sugar

⅓ cup (70g) rum or water

½ teaspoon (3g) kosher salt

2 tablespoons (15g) all-purpose flour, plus more for dusting

½ pound frozen puff pastry, thawed in the fridge overnight

Egg wash (optional): 1 large egg beaten with 1 tablespoon water

In a medium skillet, toast the pecans over medium heat, occasionally stirring, until fragrant, 5 to 6 minutes. Add the butter and cook, stirring, until the butter is melted and the pecans are fully coated, 2 to 3 minutes. Remove the pan from the heat.

Add the brown sugar, rum or water, and salt and stir to coat the buttered pecans. Add the flour and mix again to coat. Let the mixture cool completely, 15 to 20 minutes.

Line two baking sheets with parchment paper.

Dust a work surface with flour. Moving quickly to keep the puff pastry as cool as possible, roll it into a 16 × 10-inch rectangle. Using your hands or a spatula, spread the cooled pecan mixture on one long half of the pastry. Fold the pastry in half, covering the pecan filling. Press down gently with your palms to seal. Dust the top with a bit more flour and roll the folded pastry into a 19 × 7-inch rectangle, or until some of the pecans are peeking through the pastry. Trim some of the excess dough around the sides. (Sprinkle some sugar on them and bake them with the straws, cook's snack!)

If using the egg wash, use a pastry brush or your fingers to gently brush it over the top of the filled pastry. With a knife or pizza cutter, cut the rectangle the long way into 1-inch-wide straws. Twist each piece 4 to 6 times to reveal the pecan swirl. Place the twists on the baking sheets, leaving ½ inch space between them.

Loosely cover the assembled straws and refrigerate for at least 30 minutes, up to overnight. This will help the filling stay in the straws a bit more for a slightly tidier result. But you can bake these off right away as well, and any filling that melts out will form delicious, lacy edges on the straws. You can't lose either way.

Meanwhile, place an oven rack in the center of the oven. Preheat the oven to 400°F.

Note: When you pull the twists out of the oven it'll seem like you've messed up, seeing the butter-pecan filling oozing all over the tray—don't freak out because the filling will harden once cool.

Bake until the pastry is slightly puffed, crisp to the touch, and golden, 15 to 18 minutes. Carefully lift up the twists and set them aside to cool until hardened (see Note). To serve the straws, cut them in half, or keep them long and have your guests snap them. Store leftovers in an airtight container at room temperature for up to 3 days.

Smoky Spiced Eggplant Dip

Serves 4 to 6 | Prep Time: 10 minutes | Cook Time: 1 hour | Total Time: 1 hour 10 minutes

Charred eggplant simmered with garlicky spiced tomatoes—my mother makes this dip all summer long. She calls it "mayo-less eggplant salad," and while it makes more sense in Romanian, it's still a genuinely uninspired name, to be completely fair. But the taste! It certainly makes up for it. The charred eggplant smell transports me to childhood summer days. Because I grew up in a one-bedroom apartment, that aroma would flood our home in minutes. The smell was like a trigger, from that moment I had two tasks: peel the eggplant, chop it, and pass it to my mother. It was one of the first times I was allowed to use a kitchen knife. So thrilling!
   Serve with Cumin-Spiced Long Snacking Crackers (page 54) or No-Fuss Focaccia (page 65).

1 eggplant (about 1 pound)

3 tablespoons extra-virgin olive oil, plus more for drizzling

2 medium shallots, finely chopped

4 garlic cloves, finely chopped

1 teaspoon sweet paprika

1 teaspoon ground cumin

½ teaspoon freshly ground black pepper

¼ teaspoon cayenne pepper, plus more to taste

1 (14.5-ounce) can whole peeled tomatoes

Kosher salt

¼ cup chopped fresh parsley (optional), plus more for topping

½ cup whole-milk Greek yogurt

Crackers or warm bread

Heat a dry cast-iron skillet over medium heat until smoking. Place the whole eggplant in the skillet. Let the skin sear, turning from shiny purple to a muted dark brown, for 5 minutes. Turn the eggplant using tongs and repeat on another side. Continue searing and turning the eggplant until all the skin is charred and nearly flaking off, about 40 minutes total. The eggplant should feel mushy and soft. If it needs more time, don't hesitate to char it longer. Transfer the eggplant to a plate.

When the eggplant is cool enough to handle, peel off the charred skin. Set the peeled, mushy eggplant in a colander in the sink—draining off the juices will get rid of some of its bitterness. Let sit while you work on the other ingredients.

In a medium saucepan, heat the olive oil over medium heat. Add the shallots and sauté until translucent and softened, 3 to 4 minutes. Add the garlic, paprika, cumin, black pepper, and cayenne and cook just until fragrant, 1 to 2 minutes. Carefully add the tomatoes, crushing them with your hands as you add them, or using the back of a wooden spoon to break them up in the pan. Stir to combine.

Transfer the eggplant to a cutting board and chop finely. Add it to the tomato mixture in the pan, plus a hefty pinch of salt. Bring to a simmer and cook, stirring occasionally, until some of the liquid has reduced, 15 to 20 minutes. Stir in the parsley (if using), taste and adjust the seasoning. Remove the pan from the heat.

Spread the warm dip in a shallow bowl. Dollop the yogurt on top. Drizzle with olive oil, top with more parsley (if using), and another pinch of cayenne if you like. Serve with crackers or warm bread.

Flaky Spinach Artichoke Bourekas

Makes 18 bourekas | Prep Time: 30 minutes | Cook Time: 25 minutes | Total Time: 55 minutes

What if, instead of serving your favorite spinach artichoke dip in a bowl, you could trap all that cheesy gooey goodness in buttery, flaky puff pastry pockets? These bourekas are here to deliver exactly that. Bourekas are to Sephardic Jews what bagels are to Ashkenazi Jews. Bourekas are a variation of the börek, a genre of pastries and pies with Turkish origins and found in the Middle East and countries around the Mediterranean, Central Asia, and the Balkans. Israeli bourekas are typically made with puff, phyllo, or brik pastry and stuffed with anything from cheese, potatoes, or spinach to meat or sweet fillings. They make the perfect grab-and-go snack, appetizer, or lunch.

1 (10-ounce) bag frozen chopped spinach, thawed (about 1 packed cup once thawed)

1 (14-ounce) can artichoke hearts, drained and chopped

½ cup crumbled feta cheese

½ cup coarsely grated sharp cheddar cheese

3 ounces cream cheese

2 garlic cloves, finely grated or minced

Kosher salt

All-purpose flour, for dusting

1 pound frozen puff pastry, thawed in the fridge overnight

Egg wash: 1 large egg whisked with 1 tablespoon water

3 tablespoons sesame seeds (optional)

Preheat the oven to 400°F. Line two baking sheets with parchment paper.

Use your hands to squeeze out as much excess moisture from the spinach as possible. Add the spinach to a medium bowl, along with the artichokes, feta, cheddar, cream cheese, and garlic. Mix well to combine. The feta might be salty enough to season the mixture, so taste and add salt if needed.

Lightly dust a work surface with flour.

The 1 pound of pastry will either come as two 8-ounce sheets or one large 1-pound sheet. If the pastry isn't cut, slice the puff pastry in half so you're working with 8 ounces of pastry at a time. Wrap one half in plastic wrap and return it to the fridge to keep cold until you're ready to use it.

Working quickly to keep the pastry cold, roll the half of the pastry into a 12-inch square. Lightly brush a thin layer of the egg wash all over the surface. Using a knife or pizza cutter, divide the square into 9 smaller 4-inch squares.

Place just over 1 tablespoon of the spinach-artichoke filling on one side of a pastry square. Each square will be folded into a triangle along the diagonal, so nudge the filling onto one side of the diagonal. Repeat with the remaining pastry squares; you'll use about half of the filling mixture.

Fold each pastry square in half along the diagonal, gently pressing the filling into a triangle shape as you do so. Press the edges of the pastry together to enclose the filling and use your fingers or a fork to seal (see Note). If you want a perfect triangle, you can trim any excess pastry using a knife or pizza cutter. Lightly brush the top of each triangle with more egg wash. If desired, sprinkle all over with sesame seeds.

Bake until the bourekas are glossy on top and golden brown on the bottom, 25 to 28 minutes.

Repeat with the remaining pastry half and filling. Serve warm.

Note: *You can freeze them raw, right after they've been stuffed. Brush the egg wash on the the frozen bourekas, then bake them straight out of the freezer until golden and puffy, about 30 minutes.*

No-Fuss Focaccia

Makes one 9 × 13-inch loaf | Prep Time: 30 minutes, plus 10 hours proofing | Cook Time: 40 minutes | Total: 11 hours 10 minutes

While hosting guests is always an honor and a great pleasure, the week before I boarded my one-way flight to the US, it was hard to stick to my usual hostess routine. While trying to pack up my life in a suitcase and move to another continent, I found the perfect solution to hosting goodbye dinners seven days straight: focaccia!

I made a huge batch of this focaccia dough at the beginning of the week, kept it in the fridge, and each time I had guests, I'd pull out a big chunk to proof before they arrived. Day by day, the yeasty flavor got more and more irresistible. I'd bake it as soon as they'd show up, served with olive oil and vinegar, heirloom tomatoes (tossed with garlic, basil, oil, and salt), a refreshing yogurt dip, white wine, and ice cream. Such a simple, no-fuss spread that still felt thought-out and that everyone enjoyed. Ever since, I associate the aroma of freshly baked focaccia with the bittersweet taste of immigration.

1¾ cups (450g) lukewarm water

1 teaspoon (4g) active dry yeast

8 tablespoons (113g) extra-virgin olive oil, plus more as needed

4 cups (500g) all-purpose flour

2 teaspoons (10g) kosher salt

Flaky salt, for sprinkling

In a large bowl, combine the water and yeast. Set aside to let the yeast dissolve, until the water looks cloudy, about 5 minutes.

Stir 2 tablespoons (29g) of the olive oil into the yeast mixture. Add the flour and kosher salt and use oiled hands or a fork to mix until just combined, checking the bottom of the bowl for any hidden bits of dry flour. The dough will look lumpy and feel very sticky. Drizzle another 1 tablespoon (15g) oil on top, cover with a lid or plastic wrap, and refrigerate for at least 8 and up to 72 hours.

Add 2 tablespoons (29g) of the olive oil to a 9 × 13-inch baking pan (preferably metal; see Note on page 66). Spread the oil in an even layer on the bottom and sides of the pan. Turn the dough out into the pan. Oil your hands and gently press and spread the dough into an even layer to

(recipe continues)

cover most of the bottom of the pan. Cover with plastic wrap or a baking sheet and place in a warm spot until nearly doubled in size, about 2 hours. This time will largely depend on how warm your environment is, since the dough is starting out chilled, so pay more attention to how much the dough has risen rather than how much time it's taking.

Preheat the oven to 400°F.

Drizzle the remaining 3 tablespoons (40g) olive oil all over the risen dough. Using oiled hands, dimple the dough all over by gently sinking in your fingertips, moving from top to bottom and back up again. Top generously with flaky salt.

Bake until the focaccia is golden and crusty on top, 35 to 40 minutes. If the top starts browning too quickly, cover the pan with foil and continue baking as instructed.

Let cool for at least 15 minutes before slicing and serving.

Notes:

• *The best part of making focaccia—besides the dimpling—is playing around with topping variations. Have fun with it: you can sprinkle spices, seeds, nuts, fruits, and veggies on top before baking.*

• *When baking, try to avoid using ceramic or glass baking dishes because the bottom of the focaccia won't be as crispy.*

Cheesy Puff Pastry Tart
with Lemony Swiss Chard

Serves 6 to 8 | Prep Time: 30 minutes | Cook Time: 25 minutes | Total Time: 55 minutes

Judging by the number of recipes using store-bought puff pastry in this book, you'd assume I have at least five packages of puff pastry in my freezer at all times—and you'd be correct. In this recipe, we're taking the well-loved puff pastry and turning it into a base for a cheese tart. The lemony Swiss chard topping is slightly sweet, slightly bitter, and the perfect accompaniment to the custardy cheese base. I enjoy plating it up as a snackable appetizer before a hearty meal, or cut into bite-size pieces at a breakfast spread.

Lemony Chard Filling

6 large Swiss chard leaves and stems (about 1 bunch or 10 ounces); see Note

¼ cup extra-virgin olive oil

Kosher salt

6 garlic cloves, chopped

½ teaspoon Aleppo pepper or red chile flakes

2 teaspoons grated lemon zest

2 tablespoons fresh lemon juice

Cheesy Pastry Tart

All-purpose flour, for dusting

½ pound puff pastry, thawed overnight in the fridge

1 large egg

¾ cup coarsely grated low-moisture whole-milk mozzarella cheese

½ cup coarsely grated Gruyère cheese

½ cup whole-milk ricotta cheese

¼ cup crème fraîche or sour cream

Kosher salt

For Serving

Aleppo pepper or red chile flakes

Lemon zest

Flaky salt

Make the lemony chard filling: Separate the chard stems from the leaves (about 4 packed cups) and finely chop both, keeping them separated in two piles.

In a medium pan, heat the oil over medium heat. Add the chard stems and a pinch of kosher salt and cook until they are visibly softened and have faded a bit in color, 5 to 6 minutes. Add the chard leaves and cook until wilted, about 2 minutes. Add the garlic, Aleppo pepper, lemon zest, and lemon juice and cook, stirring, until fragrant, about 2 minutes. Taste and adjust the seasoning as needed. Remove the pan from the heat and let cool.

Make the cheesy pastry tart: Preheat the oven to 400°F. Line a baking sheet with parchment paper.

Lightly dust a work surface with flour and roll the puff pastry sheet into about a 9 × 13-inch rectangle just over ⅛ inch thick. If needed, use a knife or pizza cutter to trim and even out the edges. Lightly score a smaller rectangle inside the pastry, spacing it 1½ inches from the edges to create a border around the tart. Transfer the pastry to the baking sheet and use a fork to poke holes all over the inside rectangle of the pastry. (This will help the center cook through while letting the border puff up.)

Crack the egg into a large bowl and whisk until combined and uniform. Using a pastry brush or your fingers, lightly brush some of the egg over the outer border of the pastry. Set the pan in the fridge to chill while you make the cheese filling.

To the bowl with the beaten egg, add the mozzarella, Gruyère, ricotta, crème fraîche, and a big pinch of kosher salt. Stir to combine.

Note: *Not a fan of Swiss chard or can't get your hands on it? Use about 4 packed cups (10 ounces) of another seasonal leafy green or veg, such as kale, broccoli rabe, spinach, artichokes, or bright colored peppers.*

(recipe continues)

Measure ⅔ cup of the chard filling and dollop it over the inner rectangle of the pastry, using an offset or silicone spatula to spread it in an even layer. Dollop the cheese mixture over the chard, again inside the border, and evenly spread it using a spatula. Dollop the remaining chard filling over the top.

Bake until the bottom of the pastry looks golden and crusty, 25 to 30 minutes. You can use a spatula to gently lift the side of the pastry to check: If it's still soggy, give it more time; if it looks golden and flaky, it's ready to come out. If the cheese melts over the borders of the pastry, don't stress about it, it's fine. If the pastry browns too fast around the edges, loosely cover with a sheet of aluminum foil for the remainder of the cooking time.

To serve: Let cool for 5 minutes, top with Aleppo pepper, lemon zest, and flaky salt, slice, and serve warm.

Whipped Feta Dip
with Crunchy Celery and Mint

Serves 4 to 6 | Prep Time: 15 minutes | Total Time: 15 minutes

I can't get enough of feta! If you take the time to whip this cheese with a little bit of cold heavy cream in a food processor, you'll be left with this airy, spreadable, salty dip. The massaged celery topping keeps its crunch throughout serving; it's slightly sweet, a little vinegary, and the perfect contrast to the creamy dip. It makes an ideal snack for game night, a fun bite to munch on before dinner, or a great pairing to your favorite wine.

Mint Celery Topping

6 celery stalks, thinly sliced

3 tablespoons finely chopped fresh mint

1 medium jalapeño, thinly sliced (optional)

Kosher salt

¼ cup extra-virgin olive oil

2 tablespoons rice vinegar

1 tablespoon sugar

2 garlic cloves, finely chopped

Whipped Feta

2 teaspoons black peppercorns

10 ounces crumbled feta cheese (about 2 cups)

¾ cup heavy cream, plus more (see Note) if needed

Kosher salt

Fresh pita, chips, or Cumin-Spiced Long Snacking Crackers (page 54), for serving

Make the mint celery topping: In a medium bowl, combine the celery, mint, jalapeño (if using), and a big pinch of salt. Using your hands, massage the mixture until you can feel it start to soften, about 1 minute. Add the olive oil, vinegar, sugar, and garlic and toss to combine. Taste and adjust the seasoning as needed.

Make the whipped feta: In a food processor, pulse the peppercorns a few times, just to roughly grind them. Add the feta and cream and process until the mixture is smooth and creamy, about 2 minutes. Taste and adjust the seasoning as needed, knowing the feta is fairly salty but you can add more salt if you like. You can also add a splash more cream if you'd like to thin it out.

Add the whipped feta to a shallow serving bowl and create a well in the middle. Pile the fresh celery topping into the well. Serve with pita, chips, or cumin crackers.

Note: *Different fetas will come with more or less moisture in their packaging, so feel free to adjust the amount of cream accordingly.*

Smothered Sweet Onion Bread

Serves 8 to 12 | Prep time: 15 minutes | Cook time: 30 minutes | Total time: 45 minutes

Garlic bread this, garlic bread that, but have you ever tried onion bread? Imagine soft, tender layers of finely shaved yellow onion, tossed in butter with fragrant herbs. Everything melts in the oven, creating a gooey layer of soft onions, while the onion juices and butter get caught in the crusty bread. Such a reliable snacking food to serve a crowd: Cut it into small finger-size pieces so everyone can grab a hot, steamy piece. Serve on its own or with your favorite sauce, such as marinara or other dips.

1 large yellow onion (about 8 ounces), peeled

Kosher salt

8 tablespoons (4 ounces) unsalted butter, at room temperature

3 tablespoons finely chopped fresh parsley

3 garlic cloves, finely grated or minced

¼ teaspoon Aleppo pepper or red chile flakes

1 pound crusty bread, such as ciabatta or sourdough bread

Preheat the oven to 400°F. Line a baking sheet with parchment paper.

Slice the onion in half through the root end. Using a mandoline or sharp knife, very thinly slice the onion halves, aiming for less than ⅛ inch thick. Add the onion to a medium bowl and season with a hefty pinch of salt. Using your hands, squeeze and massage the salt into the onion. The onion will go from crunchy and sturdy to softened and juicy. Add the butter, parsley, garlic, and Aleppo pepper and mix until combined. Taste and add more salt if needed.

Slice the bread in half horizontally, as if you were making a giant sandwich. Place the bread halves on the baking sheet cut-sides up and spread the onion butter all over the cut sides of the bread, really piling it on.

Bake until the onions look very soft and the bread is fragrant, 30 to 35 minutes. Preheat the broiler. Place the oven rack about 4 inches from the heating element. Broil until the onions look slightly charred, 3 to 4 minutes.

Slice and serve hot.

pick a protein

One-Pan Garlicky Chicken Couscous

Serves 4 to 6 | Prep Time: 15 minutes | Cook Time: 1 hour | Total Time: 1 hour 15 minutes

While most people grew up with chicken and rice, in my home, pearled couscous was the go-to grain pairing for chicken. This one-pot no-fuss meal is my take on a dinner my mother used to make for any picky eaters visiting us. The chicken gets seared until golden and crispy, the couscous is toasted in the rendered schmaltz. Stir in the secret ingredient—chicken bouillon for that ultimate chicken-soup flavor—then steam it all in the oven. Finish the chicken dinner with a bright, herby sauce for some extra freshness.

Garlicky Chicken and Couscous

4 to 6 bone-in, skin-on chicken thighs (1½ to 2 pounds total)

Kosher salt and freshly ground black pepper

3 tablespoons neutral oil, such as sunflower or grapeseed

2 medium shallots, finely sliced

1½ cups pearled (Israeli) couscous or orzo

15 garlic cloves, lightly crushed and peeled

1 chicken bouillon cube or 2 teaspoons chicken bouillon powder

Dill Topping

⅓ cup chopped fresh dill

⅓ cup brined capers, drained, rinsed, and finely chopped

3 tablespoons extra-virgin olive oil

2 tablespoons rice vinegar or apple cider vinegar

3 garlic cloves, finely grated or minced

1 teaspoon red chile flakes, plus more to taste

Kosher salt and freshly ground black pepper

Make the garlicky chicken and couscous: Preheat the oven to 425°F.

Using a paper towel, pat the chicken thighs dry. Season generously on all sides with salt and pepper.

In a 12-inch cast-iron or other ovenproof skillet, heat 1 tablespoon of the oil over medium heat. Add the chicken skin-side down and cook until the skin looks golden and crisp, and releases easily from the pan, 6 to 8 minutes. If the chicken skin sticks when you try to flip it, it just needs more time to crisp. Flip and cook until golden, 4 to 5 minutes. Transfer the chicken to a plate.

Add the remaining 2 tablespoons oil and the shallots to the hot pan and cook until the shallots are slightly softened, about 2 minutes. Add the couscous and continue cooking, stirring occasionally, until it's fragrant and turning a toasty brown color, 4 to 5 minutes. Add 3 cups water, the garlic, chicken bouillon, and a hefty pinch of salt. Arrange the chicken thighs on top, crispy skin-side up. Increase the heat to medium-high and bring to a simmer. Remove the pan from the heat.

Carefully cover the hot pan with aluminum foil, pinching around the sides to create a tight seal. Transfer to the oven and bake until most of the liquid has been absorbed, 30 to 35 minutes.

Meanwhile, make the dill topping: In a small bowl, stir together the dill, capers, oil, vinegar, garlic, chile flakes, and salt and black pepper to taste.

Remove the foil from the chicken and bake for another 5 minutes. Preheat the broiler. Place the oven rack about 4 inches from the heating element. Broil until the chicken skin becomes crispy, 2 to 3 minutes. Remove from the oven. Fish out the softened garlic cloves and crush them on top of the crispy chicken thighs.

Dollop the dill topping all over the hot chicken couscous and serve right away.

Spiced Kebabs
with Mint Sauce and Pineapple

Serves 4 | Prep Time: 15 minutes | Cook Time: 15 minutes | Total Time: 30 minutes

Ground meat is one of the cheapest, most versatile proteins you could get your hands on. You'll always find some in my freezer, ready to be thawed for dinner at any moment, like for these kebabs. If you've never made kebabs before, they might seem ridiculously intimidating to make at home. I'm here to tell you they're as easy to make as a burger—if you can pack spiced meat on a skewer and roast it for a handful of minutes, you've got dinner covered.

Now, pineapple on pizza might be controversial, but pineapple on meat? It contributes the perfect amount of tartness and sweetness to complement any hearty protein. Roasting the pineapple as the spiced kebab meat drips over it will flavor the fruit, soften its texture, and make it extra succulent. It all gets topped with a fresh mint sauce, a perfect pairing for lamb and beef due to its bold, fresh aroma and pleasant bitterness.

Kebabs

1 small pineapple

1 pound ground beef (80/20) or ground lamb

4 garlic cloves, minced or finely grated

3 tablespoons finely chopped fresh parsley

1 teaspoon ground cumin

½ teaspoon sweet paprika

¼ teaspoon ground cinnamon

¼ teaspoon ground turmeric

¼ teaspoon cayenne pepper

Kosher salt

Mint Sauce

1 cup finely chopped fresh mint leaves

4 garlic cloves, minced or finely grated

2 small shallots, thinly sliced

Grated zest and juice of 2 limes

Kosher salt

½ cup extra-virgin olive oil

Warm pitas, for serving

Make the kebabs: Preheat the oven to 425°F.

Peel and core the pineapple, then cut half into 6 to 8 long wedges (save the rest for snacking). Set the pineapple wedges in a 9 × 13-inch baking pan.

In a medium bowl, combine the beef, garlic, parsley, cumin, paprika, cinnamon, turmeric, cayenne, and a big pinch of salt. Using your hands or a silicone spatula, mix until just combined.

Divide the mixture into 6 even portions. Wet your dominant hand with a bit of water and grab one portion of the meat mixture. Lay a long (10 inches or more) wooden or metal skewer (see Note) across the meat and use your wet hand to gradually shape it into a 7- to 9-inch sausage shape around the skewer. Lay the skewer widthwise across the baking pan, setting the ends of the skewer on the edges of the pan so the meat is suspended over the pineapple. Repeat with the remaining meat mixture.

Bake the skewers until cooked through and fragrant, 8 to 10 minutes.

Preheat the broiler. Place the oven rack about 4 inches from the heating element. Broil the skewers until slightly caramelized on top, 2 to 3 minutes. Set aside to cool slightly.

Make the mint sauce: In a small bowl, combine the mint, garlic, shallots, lime zest, lime juice, and a pinch of salt and mix, crushing the garlic and shallot with the back of a spoon as you go. Add the oil and stir again to combine. Taste and adjust the salt as needed.

To serve, slide the meat off the skewers and place it right on the warm pita. Add a wedge of the roasted pineapple and drizzle some of the drippings on top. Spoon the mint sauce on top and serve.

Note: *If you don't have any skewers, you could shape the meat by hand into a sausage-like shape and place it directly on the baking pan, over the pineapple. Carefully flip them halfway through cooking.*

Chicken Schnitzel
with Caramelized Lemon Gremolata

Serves 4 to 6 | Prep time: 40 minutes, plus 20 minutes chilling | Cook time: 15 minutes |
Total time: 1 hour 15 minutes

Something magical happens when you take any piece of meat, coat it in bread crumbs, and fry it to perfection: juicy and hot on the inside, golden brown and crunchy on the outside. It's so simple, yet every bite is a thrill. Schnitzels are often served with a lemon wedge to level out richness, so let's take that a step further with a vibrant, caramelized lemon gremolata. During the searing process, the lemons develop so much complexity. They get slightly sweet and toffee-like and a little bitter from the char.

Marinated Chicken

6 boneless, skinless chicken breasts (about 3 pounds)

2 teaspoons kosher salt

1 teaspoon black pepper

½ chicken stock cube, crumbled, or ½ teaspoon bouillon powder (optional)

¼ teaspoon cayenne pepper

1 tablespoon hot sauce (optional)

Caramelized Lemon Gremolata

4 small Meyer or regular lemons (see page 21)

4 tablespoons extra-virgin olive oil, plus more to taste

¾ cup finely chopped parsley

3 scallions, thinly sliced

3 garlic cloves, grated

2 serrano chiles, thinly sliced

Kosher salt

Chicken Schnitzel

2¼ cups all-purpose flour

1 teaspoon kosher salt

3 large eggs

½ teaspoon black pepper

Hot sauce (optional)

2¼ cups panko or other bread crumbs

¼ cup sesame seeds

Neutral oil for shallow-frying

Flaky salt

Marinate the chicken: Use a paper towel to pat dry the chicken breasts. Cut each chicken breast in half lengthwise to create 2 thin cutlets. Slice each chicken cutlet in half, at an angle, widthwise (see Note).

Place a few chicken pieces in a zip-seal plastic bag. Place the bag on a cutting board and use a rolling pin to pound each cutlet to about ¼ inch thick. Set the pounded cutlets on a baking sheet and repeat with the remaining cutlets.

In a small bowl, combine the kosher salt, pepper, the crumbled chicken stock cube (if using), and the cayenne. Sprinkle the mixture all over both sides of the cutlets. If using hot sauce, drizzle it over the cutlets. Marinate the chicken at room temperature for 15 to 20 minutes, or up to 8 hours in the fridge.

Make the caramelized lemon gremolata: Gently scrub the Meyer lemons under warm running water. Using a sharp knife, cut both ends off 2 lemons. (You'll use the ends later.) Slice the lemons as thinly as you can manage, about ⅛ inch thick.

In a large skillet, heat 2 tablespoons of the oil over medium heat. Carefully add about half of the lemon slices to the pan and let them sear, mostly undisturbed, until amber and caramelized, 5 to 7 minutes. Using a pair of tongs, carefully flip the lemon slices and sear again. The second side won't take quite as long, maybe 3 or 5 minutes, but be sure to keep a close eye, as the natural sugars can burn quite quickly. Return the seared lemon slices to the cutting board. Add the remaining 2 tablespoons oil to the skillet and repeat with the remaining half of the lemon slices. Transfer the seared slices to the board.

Note: *This recipe won't yield huge, butterflied schnitzels. The cutting method is an ode to my mother's way of stretching the chicken breast to as many servings as possible. I will always remember the pile of small schnitzels waiting for us on the dinner table.*

(recipe continues)

Cut the remaining 2 lemons in half (as if you were getting them ready to juice). Add the 4 lemon halves to the pan and sear until they develop char marks. Remove the pan from the heat and reserve the lemon halves for serving.

Using one of the reserved lemon ends, rub the skillet with the cut side of the lemon to break up the browned and caramelized lemon bits on the bottom of the pan. Use a spatula to scrape all the bits and any oil and juice into a bowl. Chop the seared lemon slices into a rough paste and add to the bowl along with the parsley, scallions, garlic, chiles, and a big pinch of kosher salt. Taste and add more salt, lemon juice, or olive oil as needed.

Cook the schnitzel: Prepare a dredging station in three shallow medium bowls: Combine the flour and ½ teaspoon of the kosher salt in one. In a second, whisk together the eggs, remaining ½ teaspoon salt, the black pepper, and a few shakes of hot sauce (if using). In a third bowl, toss together the panko and sesame seeds.

Working with one cutlet at a time, dip it in the flour, followed by the egg mixture, and finally in the sesame/panko, pressing it into the panko to ensure an even coating. Transfer to a baking sheet or plate and repeat with the remaining cutlets.

Line a baking sheet with paper towels and set a rack on top and set near the stove. Pour 1 inch of oil into a large, deep frying pan and heat the oil over medium-high heat to 375°F.

Fry each schnitzel until crispy and golden brown all over, 3 to 4 minutes per side, reducing the heat as needed. Transfer the crispy schnitzel to the rack and season with flaky salt. Repeat with the remaining schnitzel.

Serve the schnitzel right away topped with spoonfuls of the lemon gremolata and squeezes of lemon juice from the charred lemon halves.

Creamy Peanut Butter Chicken Mafé–Inspired Stew

Serves 4 to 6 | Prep Time: 15 minutes | Cook Time: 1 hour 10 minutes | Total Time: 1 hour 25 minutes

Chicken mafé, a West African creamy chicken stew, is traditionally served over a large platter, accompanied by savory grains, root vegetables, and chunky cabbage wedges. I first encountered this dish watching chef Pierre Thiam share his version of the stew. It looked so irresistible, I re-created it for dinner that very night. Ever since, this has become a crowd favorite in the Gelen kitchen.

My version draws inspiration from the classic, but further maximizes its spoonability: I finely grate the veggies and cook them right in the gingery stew. I skip the bone-in meat and use cubed chicken thighs instead, but to replicate that comforting bone broth flavor, I sneak in a cube of chicken bouillon.

3 tablespoons neutral oil, such as sunflower or grapeseed

1½ pounds boneless, skinless chicken thighs, cut into 1-inch cubes

Kosher salt and freshly ground black pepper

1 medium yellow onion, finely chopped

6 garlic cloves, finely chopped

1-inch knob fresh ginger, grated (no need to peel), about 1½ tablespoons

1 red Fresno chile, thinly sliced, plus more for serving

1 teaspoon red chile flakes

2 tablespoons tomato paste

1 chicken bouillon cube or 2 teaspoons chicken bouillon powder

½ cup creamy peanut butter, can be natural or processed (see Note)

2 cups finely sliced green cabbage (about ¼ small head)

1 medium Yukon Gold potato, coarsely grated

1 medium carrot, coarsely grated

Hot cooked rice, for serving

Fresh cilantro (optional), for serving

In a large saucepan, heat 1 tablespoon of the oil over medium-high heat. Add the chicken and season generously with salt and pepper. Cook, stirring occasionally, until browned on all sides, 10 to 12 minutes.

Move the chicken to one side of the pan and add the remaining 2 tablespoons oil. Add the onion and cook, stirring occasionally, until softened and translucent, 5 to 6 minutes. If the bottom of the pot starts to burn, add a splash of water to deglaze the pan. Stir to combine the cooked onions with the chicken.

Add the garlic, ginger, fresh chile, and chile flakes and cook until fragrant, about 2 minutes. Add the tomato paste and cook, stirring frequently, until it darkens to a deep red, 2 to 3 minutes. Add a splash of water as needed to prevent the tomato paste from scorching. Add 3 cups water, the chicken bouillon, and a hefty pinch of salt. Bring to a boil, reduce the heat to medium-low, and simmer for 10 minutes.

In a heatproof medium bowl, stir about ¼ cup of the hot broth into the peanut butter and whisk until smooth. Repeat 3 more times, adding ¼ cup of hot broth at a time to the peanut butter and whisking until smooth. Slowly add the peanut butter mixture back to the pan, stirring constantly. Continue simmering the stew for 20 minutes, stirring occasionally.

Add the cabbage, potato, and carrot and simmer until the cabbage is tender, 10 to 15 minutes. Taste and adjust the seasoning, adding more salt or chile flakes as needed.

Serve the hot, creamy stew over rice and top with sliced red chiles and cilantro (if using).

Note: *Concerning peanut butter types, a processed peanut butter will give you a better emulsion, with a bit of a sweeter taste, which I really enjoy, whereas the all-natural peanut butter brings an earthier flavor. Both are great, so use whichever one you have on hand! If your sauce splits, a tablespoon of cornstarch mixed with a little bit of water will bring it back together.*

Lemon Pepper Roast Chicken
with Schmaltz Potatoes

Serves 4 to 6 | Prep Time: 35 minutes | Cook Time: 1 hour | Total Time: 1 hour 35 minutes

This book wouldn't have been complete without a showstopping roasted chicken recipe. Whether you're feeding a crowd or making dinner for two, it's hard to go wrong with a delicious roasted chicken. I wanted to share a version of my mother's infamous roast. Her secret? Seasoning the chicken with a crumbled bouillon cube for the chicken-iest flavor. We're keeping everything else simple: some turmeric for an irresistible yellow color, sharp, crunchy peppercorns, and a little bit of garlic.

If you're roasting a whole chicken, you might as well throw some veggies underneath to absorb all the schmaltzy drippings. We're roasting some potatoes alongside the chicken, while the lemon at the bottom of the pan melts in the schmaltz. Your kitchen is going to smell incredible!

Schmaltz Potatoes

1½ pounds baby gold potatoes, halved

1 large yellow onion, cut into 8 wedges

2 small Meyer or regular lemons (see page 21), cut into 8 wedges each, seeds removed

2 tablespoons extra-virgin olive oil

½ tablespoon coarsely cracked black pepper

Kosher salt

Roasted Chicken

1 whole chicken (3½ to 4 pounds)

Kosher salt

5 tablespoons extra-virgin olive oil

1 tablespoon chicken bouillon powder or 1 chicken bouillon cube, crushed

2 teaspoons coarsely cracked black pepper

6 garlic cloves, minced or finely grated

1 teaspoon ground turmeric

Preheat the oven to 425°F.

Prepare the potatoes: In a 9 × 13-inch roasting pan, combine the potatoes, onion, lemons, olive oil, cracked pepper, and a big pinch of salt. Toss to coat everything in the oil. Push the lemons in the middle, tucking them underneath the potatoes to ensure they stay submerged and infuse the schmaltz.

Spatchcock the chicken: This isn't the prettiest thing you'll do in the kitchen, but spatchcocking the chicken will be worth it. Remove the neck or giblets (if any) from the chicken cavity (you can roast them here or freeze for use in stock). Using paper towels, pat the chicken dry.

Place the chicken breast-side down on a large cutting board, with the tail-bone facing you. Using a pair of strong kitchen shears and a little elbow grease, cut along the right side of the backbone, all the way up toward the neck. Now cut along the left side of the backbone and remove the backbone completely (you can roast the backbone here or freeze it with the other scraps for stock).

Flip the chicken breast-side up, loosely pulling out the thighs and wings. Position your palms over the center of the chicken. Channel your inner chiropractor and crack the wishbone: Press down on the chicken breast until you hear a crack and the chicken seems a little flatter. Pull the thighs out to the sides of the chicken, trimming any extra skin if needed. Use a paring knife or skewer to poke the chicken skin all over to help the fat render out evenly.

From a height, generously season both sides of the chicken with salt. Place the chicken over the potatoes, skin-side down, cavity-side up, and set aside while working on the marinades.

(recipe continues)

In a small bowl, stir together 3 tablespoons of the olive oil, the chicken bouillon, and the cracked black pepper. In another small bowl, stir together the remaining 2 tablespoons olive oil, the garlic, and the turmeric.

Brush a small amount of the bouillon/black pepper oil all over the chicken cavity, saving most of it for the other side. Flip the chicken skin-side up and brush the remaining bouillon/black pepper oil all over the skin, in all crevices. Twist and tuck the wing tips underneath the breast to prevent them from burning. Pull out the chicken thighs so they're not tucked in underneath the breast.

Roast until the chicken skin is lightly golden but not yet crisp, 20 to 25 minutes. Remove from the oven and brush the garlic/turmeric oil all over the chicken. Spoon some of the chicken fat and juices all over the chicken. Return to the oven and roast for 10 to 15 minutes. The skin should look crispy and slightly charred. Loosely cover the chicken with foil and continue baking until the internal temperature of the chicken breast measures 165°F, 10 to 20 minutes, depending on the size of your chicken.

Remove the chicken from the oven and let rest for 10 to 15 minutes. Carve the chicken and transfer to a serving platter. Spoon the tender lemon pieces all over the chicken. (Alternatively, chop the lemon and mix it with more of the schmaltz from the pan before spooning.) Serve with the roasted potatoes and onion.

Note: *Looking for ways to use up the leftover roasted chicken? Try my Miso Mushroom Chicken Soup (page 172).*

Sweet and Spicy Baked Wings

Serves 4 | Prep Time: 10 minutes | Cook Time: 50 minutes | Total Time: 1 hour

I always viewed saucy wings as this ultra-American food. The only way I'd eaten wings before moving to the US was roasted or grilled, never coated in sauce, and maybe served with mustard on the side. I remember having wings for the first time in the US and my American friends were shocked at how clean I left the bones on my plate. Apparently some children don't get bullied into finishing the meat off their bones—must be nice! I remember as a child, a parent or relative would check your plate and eat the meat you left on your bones, while nodding at you in disapproval. That's one way to teach little ones about food waste!

Wings may be commonly viewed as an appetizer, but to me, they're full-on dinner. This portion serves four as an appetizer and two as a dinner. They're salty, savory, garlicky and it's hard to keep yourself from going in for more.

Chicken Wings

3 pounds chicken wings (separated into drummettes and flats)

1 tablespoon baking powder

Kosher salt

¼ cup neutral oil, such as sunflower or grapeseed

Sweet and Spicy Sauce

2 teaspoons crushed Aleppo pepper or red chile flakes

½ cup honey

¼ cup hot sauce, plus more to taste

2 tablespoons soy sauce, plus more to taste

6 to 10 garlic cloves, finely grated or minced

4 tablespoons chopped fresh chives, for serving

Make the chicken wings: Preheat the oven to 425°F. Line a baking sheet with parchment paper.

Pat the chicken wings thoroughly dry with a paper towel. Add them to a large bowl, along with the baking powder and a big pinch of salt. Toss well to coat. Add the oil and toss again until the wings are evenly coated. Spread the wings evenly on the baking sheet, leaving a bit of space between the pieces.

Bake the wings until crispy, with a few bubbles in their crust, 45 to 50 minutes.

Transfer the wings to a serving bowl, reserving the chicken fat in the baking sheet.

Make the sweet and spicy sauce: Pour the chicken fat from the baking sheet into a medium saucepan (see Note). Add the Aleppo pepper and cook over medium heat for 30 seconds to 1 minute, just until the fat turns orange. Add the honey, hot sauce, and soy sauce and cook until slightly thickened, 4 to 5 minutes. Remove the pan from the heat and add the garlic, dragging it around in the warm sauce for a minute or so, just until fragrant.

Add the crispy wings to the sauce and toss to coat. Carefully taste and add more hot sauce or soy sauce if you like. Top with the fresh chives and serve right away.

Note: *We will be tossing the wings in this pot later, so choose the medium size accordingly.*

Not-to-Brag-but-the-Best Short Rib Stew

Serves 4 | Prep Time: 20 minutes | Cook Time: 3 hours 40 minutes | Total Time: 4 hours

Beautifully marbled short ribs seared to perfection, nestled in a spiced, veggie-heavy broth sweetened with prunes and red wine, and gently cooked till the meat falls off the bone—how comforting does that sound?! Prunes are my secret ingredient in this delicious stew. During the process of drying plums to make prunes, the fruit develops a concentrated yet subtle sweetness, a jammy texture, and earthy, chocolaty undertones. That wonderful flavor profile seeps into our stew, coating the fall-off-the-bone ribs in a rich, silky, deep burgundy sauce. Every time I serve this, I like having my guests guess the secret ingredient, and have yet to find someone who discovers the answer without any hints. If you can't get your hands on prunes, dried apricots or dates will lead you to a similar result.

This stew is incredible served over pappardelle pasta or even just alongside some crusty bread and a green salad.

2 tablespoons neutral oil, such as sunflower or grapeseed

3 pounds bone-in beef short ribs

Kosher salt

3 medium carrots, cut into 1-inch chunks

12 celery stalks (about 1 bunch), roughly chopped

5 medium shallots, roughly chopped

3 tablespoons tomato paste

1 tablespoon black peppercorns

1 tablespoon cumin seeds

2 teaspoons coriander seeds

½ teaspoon cayenne pepper

3 cups red wine

2 heaping cups prunes (about 14 ounces)

2 small garlic heads, top cut off, root attached

1 cinnamon stick (optional)

Chopped fresh parsley or chives, for serving

Preheat the oven to 350°F.

In a large Dutch oven or other heavy-bottomed ovenproof pot, heat the oil over medium heat. Generously season the short ribs all over with salt. Working in batches, sear the short ribs on all sides, until each side has developed a dark brown crust, 3 to 4 minutes per side. Transfer the seared ribs to a plate.

In the same pot, cook the carrots, celery, shallots, and a big pinch of salt over medium-high heat, stirring occasionally, until the vegetables are softened and less vibrant, 20 to 25 minutes. If the bottom of the pan starts to burn, add a splash of water to deglaze it.

Add the tomato paste, peppercorns, cumin seeds, coriander seeds, and cayenne and stir to coat the vegetables. Cook, stirring frequently, until the tomato paste turns a rich burgundy color, 4 to 6 minutes. Stir in the wine, prunes, garlic heads, cinnamon stick (if using), 3 cups water, and a big pinch of salt. Using tongs, add the short ribs, submerging them in the liquid.

Cover the pot, transfer to the oven, and bake for 3 hours. The meat will be super tender and should come away from the bone easily.

Using tongs, carefully transfer the short ribs to a plate. Set a fine-mesh strainer over a large bowl. Strain out the vegetables and whole spices and discard the solids. You'll be left with a delicious, dark brown gravy (see Note).

Spoon the gravy over the short ribs, top with the fresh herbs, and serve.

Note: *I like to serve the gravy as is, but if you'd like it a little thicker, simmer it in a pot for 8 to 10 minutes over medium heat to reduce it.*

Think Cabbage Roll in a Casserole

Serves 6 to 8 | Prep Time: 25 minutes | Cook Time: 2 hours 30 minutes | Total Time: 2 hours 55 minutes

If you grew up with cabbage rolls, you appreciate how long they take to make. Not only do you have to make the meaty rice filling, steam the cabbage, prepare the leaves, you have to roll hundreds—yes, hundreds—of tiny rolls. In Romania, home cooks take pride in how small they can roll them; the gold standard is rolls as small as a thumb. I remember my mother receiving calls from relatives, who bragged about how many they'd rolled in a day like it was a competition: "I made 154 rolls!" "Oh, that's nothing, I rolled 237!"

My recipe removes the rolling process, the lengthiest, fussiest part, and instead, layers the cabbage and spiced meat like building a lasagna. The cabbage is baked to perfection in tangy tomato juices, making an impressive centerpiece for any celebratory gathering.

1 small head green cabbage (about 2 pounds)

4 tablespoons neutral oil, such as sunflower or grapeseed, plus more for greasing and drizzling

2 medium shallots, finely chopped

½ cup long-grain white rice, thoroughly rinsed and drained

1 heaping tablespoon tomato paste

8 garlic cloves, finely chopped

1 tablespoon sweet paprika

2 teaspoons chopped fresh thyme leaves or 1 teaspoon dried thyme

1 teaspoon freshly ground black pepper

1 teaspoon cayenne pepper

1 pound ground beef (80/20)

Kosher salt

1 (28-ounce) can tomato sauce

1 (14.5-ounce) can whole peeled tomatoes

Preheat the oven to 400°F.

Slice the cabbage in half, through the stem. Tightly wrap the cabbage halves in aluminum foil, place on a baking sheet, and bake until super soft and tender all the way through, 45 to 50 minutes. Set aside to cool but leave the oven on.

In a medium skillet, heat 3 tablespoons of the oil over medium heat. Add the shallots and cook, stirring frequently, until softened and translucent, 4 to 5 minutes. Add the rice and cook, stirring, until toasted and fragrant, another 4 to 5 minutes. Add the tomato paste and cook, stirring to coat the rice in the tomato paste, until the mixture darkens and begins to caramelize on the bottom of the pan, about 3 minutes.

Create a space in the middle of the pan and add the remaining 1 tablespoon oil, plus the garlic, paprika, thyme, black pepper, and cayenne. Cook until very fragrant, about 2 minutes. Add the beef and a big pinch of salt and mix well to incorporate the spices into the beef. (We're looking to use the warmth in the pan to help break up the beef and cook it a little, but not all the way through, since it will cook in the oven.) Remove the pan from the heat.

Add all of the tomato sauce and the whole tomatoes, crushing them with your hands as you add them to the beef mixture. Add a few tablespoons of water to each of the cans to swish around and pick up whatever tomato sauce is still in the can. Add that to the pan and stir to combine. This will look like a weird raw ragu, but remember, this is all getting baked together with the cabbage. Trust the process!

To assemble the cabbage roll cake, grease a deep 10-inch springform pan (see Note) with oil. Line a baking sheet with parchment paper and set the springform on the baking sheet.

Note: *You can also use a regular 10-inch round pan, though the cabbage roll cake will be harder to remove from the pan. If you go that route, instead of struggling to flip the cake and pull it out onto a serving platter, simply serve it straight out of the pan.*

(recipe continues)

Add a dollop of the tomato-beef mixture to the bottom of the pan and spread it in an even layer. Pull off about one-fourth of the leaves from the steamed cabbage. Chop any thicker cabbage core pieces and save them for the final layer. Layer the cabbage leaves over the sauce, letting them overlap as needed to fully cover the sauce.

Add a third of the tomato-beef mixture over the cabbage, followed by another fourth of the cabbage leaves in an even layer. Add another third of the tomato-beef mixture and top with another fourth of the cabbage leaves in an even layer.

Top with the remaining third of the tomato sauce, followed by the remaining fourth of the cabbage leaves, including the chopped cabbage cores on top.

Tightly cover the pan with foil and bake for 1 hour and 20 minutes.

Carefully remove the foil and drizzle the cabbage with a few tablespoons of oil. Continue to bake until the top layer of cabbage is golden brown, about 15 more minutes.

Preheat the broiler. Place the oven rack about 4 inches from the heating element. Broil until the cabbage is nicely charred, 3 to 4 minutes.

Let cool for 10 to 15 minutes before serving. Slice and serve like you would a lasagna or a cake. The reference photo stacks cabbage roll cakes; your cake should be half as tall.

Tuna Burgers with Yogurt-Dill Sauce

Serves 4 to 6 | Prep Time: 20 minutes, plus 15 minutes chilling | Cook Time: 10 minutes | Total Time: 45 minutes

Listen, I'm a tuna gal through and through. I enjoy diving into a lemony tuna salad, I'm all in for a tuna melt, and look forward to having tuna cakes for dinner. These burgers made with canned tuna are packed with protein and will keep you full for a while. While the ingredient list might seem never-ending, I promise you the recipe is very adaptable to your pantry. Not a fan of turmeric? Omit it. Hate capers? Leave them out. Can't get behind cayenne pepper? Use sweet paprika instead. Don't be afraid to work with what you have and embrace the final result your kitchen is creating.

Yogurt-Dill Sauce

1 cup whole-milk Greek yogurt

3 garlic cloves, minced or grated

2 tablespoons chopped fresh dill

2 teaspoons fresh lemon juice

Kosher salt

Tuna Patties (see Note)

2 large eggs

¼ cup chopped fresh parsley

4 garlic cloves, minced or grated

3 tablespoons neutral oil, such as sunflower or grapeseed

1 medium shallot, finely chopped

2 tablespoons brined capers, rinsed and finely chopped

Grated zest of 1 medium lemon

1 tablespoon fresh lemon juice

1 teaspoon onion powder

1 teaspoon ground turmeric

¼ teaspoon cayenne pepper

Kosher salt and freshly ground black pepper

3 (5-ounce) cans solid albacore tuna, drained

½ cup panko or other bread crumbs

½ cup all-purpose flour, plus more as needed

For Serving

Neutral, oil, such as sunflower or grapeseed, for the pan

Hamburger buns, split

Any burger toppings you like, such as cheese, pickles, sliced tomatoes, crisp lettuce, etc.

Make the yogurt-dill sauce: In a small bowl, whisk together the yogurt, garlic, dill, lemon juice, and a pinch of salt.

Make the tuna patties: In a medium bowl, combine the eggs, parsley, garlic, oil, shallot, capers, lemon zest, lemon juice, onion powder, turmeric, cayenne, a big pinch of salt, and several grinds of black pepper. Whisk well to combine. Add the tuna, panko, and flour and gently mix using your hands or a silicone spatula, flaking the tuna into smaller pieces. If the mixture is hard to shape into a patty, add a couple of extra tablespoons of flour. Set aside for 15 minutes.

To serve: Place a well-seasoned cast-iron or nonstick skillet over medium heat. Heat a drizzle of oil for 2 to 3 minutes. Divide the tuna mixture into 6 equal portions. Using your hands, form one portion into a ball. Gently flatten the ball into a patty and place it in the hot pan. Cook until the underside is crisp and golden, 2 to 3 minutes. Flip and cook for 2 to 3 minutes more. Transfer to a plate or rack. Repeat with the remaining tuna mixture, adjusting the heat as needed.

Add a dollop of the yogurt sauce to the bottom of a bun, followed by a tuna patty. Top with your favorite toppings, one more dollop of yogurt, and the top bun.

Note: *I know this ingredient list might look a little lengthy, but a good chunk of it is just spices. If you can't find all these spices in your pantry, substitute them with other spices you have on hand.*

Spiced Tomato Stew
with Poached Salmon and Olives

Serves 4 | Prep Time: 15 minutes | Cook Time: 40 minutes | Total Time: 55 minutes

Delicate, flaky salmon poached in a tart, spiced tomato sauce with briny capers and olives—this elegant dish makes me feel like I'm having dinner, midsummer, at sunset in a small seaside town. The fresh flavors paired with a glass of dry sparkling white wine and some warm crusty bread have the capacity to transport you there. This recipe is inspired by a stew from my favorite Afghan restaurant; they smoke their fish over charcoal and it's just oh-so-memorable.

3 tablespoons extra-virgin olive oil

2 small yellow onions, thinly sliced

Kosher salt

4 garlic cloves, minced or grated

1 teaspoon ground turmeric

1 teaspoon sweet paprika

½ teaspoon freshly ground black pepper, plus more to taste

¼ teaspoon cayenne pepper, plus more to taste

1 cup lukewarm water

1 (14.5-ounce) can whole peeled tomatoes

1 pound skinless salmon fillets (2 to 3 fillets)

1 cup brined unpitted Castelvetrano olives (see Note), drained

¼ cup brined capers, drained

Crusty bread, such as focaccia (see page 65), ciabatta, or sourdough bread, for serving

In a medium pot, heat the oil over medium heat. Add the onions and a pinch of salt and cook, stirring occasionally, until the onions are very soft and slightly browned on the edges, about 10 minutes. If the onions are browning too fast, add a splash of water and reduce the heat to medium-low, scraping any browned bits from the bottom of the pot.

Stir in the garlic, turmeric, paprika, black pepper, and cayenne and cook until just fragrant, 1 or 2 minutes. Add the water and canned tomatoes to the pot, crushing the tomatoes with your hands as you're adding them or breaking them up in the pot with a wooden spoon. Season with a hefty pinch of salt, increase the heat to medium-high, and bring the mixture to a boil. Reduce the heat to medium-low and simmer uncovered, stirring occasionally, until slightly reduced, about 10 minutes.

Add the salmon fillets, nestling them into the poaching liquid, and reduce the heat to low. Partially cover and gently simmer until the fish is cooked through and flakes easily with a fork, about 15 minutes. Remove the pot from the heat.

Using a pair of forks, flake the fish into smaller chunks. Add the olives and capers and stir gently to combine. Taste and adjust the seasoning as needed.

Divide the stew among bowls and serve with warm bread on the side.

Note: *Castelvetrano olives are ideal for this dish. They're buttery, crisp, meaty, and mild in flavor, and they add a lot to the recipe without overpowering the sauce. Other varieties I tested, such as kalamata, Mission, and Manzanilla, tended to clash with this dish's flavor profile. And make sure you're using whole olives; pitted olives tend to be mushier, saltier, and significantly less flavorful compared to whole olives.*

Crispy Coconut Chicken Bites
with Pineapple-Basil Salsa

Serves 4 | Prep Time: 30 minutes, plus 15 minutes chilling | Cook Time: 25 minutes | Total Time: 1 hour 10 minutes

Chicken nuggets, but a little more tropical! These coconut-coated chicken bites come in handy for any weeknight meal. While the nuggets are roasting, whip together a tart, refreshing salsa with pineapple and lots of torn fresh basil. Smother the coconutty bites in the pineapple salsa with all of its juices and you've got yourself a delicious dinner.

Marinated Chicken

3 tablespoons neutral oil, such as sunflower or grapeseed

4 garlic cloves, finely grated

3 tablespoons cornstarch

1 large egg white

1 tablespoon rice vinegar

1½ teaspoons onion powder

1½ teaspoons baking powder

1 teaspoon sweet paprika

¼ teaspoon cayenne pepper

Kosher salt

1½ pounds boneless, skinless chicken thighs, cut into 1-inch pieces

Pineapple-Basil Salsa

1½ cups finely diced fresh pineapple (about 10 ounces)

1 cup packed fresh basil leaves, torn into small pieces

3 tablespoons extra-virgin olive oil, optional (see Note)

Grated zest and juice of 2 limes

Kosher salt

Crispy Coconut Chicken

2 cups sweetened coconut flakes

1½ cups panko or other bread crumbs

3 tablespoons neutral oil, such as sunflower or grapeseed

Kosher salt

Flaky salt

Marinate the chicken: In a medium bowl, whisk together the oil, garlic, cornstarch, egg white, vinegar, onion powder, baking powder, paprika, cayenne, and a big pinch of kosher salt. Add the chicken and toss to coat. Marinate for 15 minutes.

Make the pineapple-basil salsa: In a medium bowl, toss together the pineapple, basil, olive oil, lime zest, lime juice, and a pinch of kosher salt, gently crushing some of the pineapple with the back of the spoon as you mix.

Make the crispy coconut chicken: Preheat the oven to 400°F. Line a baking sheet with parchment paper.

In a medium bowl, add the coconut flakes, panko, and neutral oil and stir to combine.

Dip a piece of the marinated chicken in the coconut/panko mixture, pressing down to help the coating stick on all sides. Add the chicken to the baking sheet and repeat with the remaining chicken, leaving about 1 inch between the chicken pieces.

Bake until the chicken is golden brown on top, about 15 minutes. Using a pair of tongs, flip the chicken pieces and bake until golden and crispy all over, 8 to 10 more minutes. Season the chicken with a pinch of kosher salt.

Serve the crispy chicken warm or at room temperature (see Note), topped with the pineapple-basil salsa and flaky salt.

Notes:

• *Oil in salsa? Crazy, I know! It's something I like to call not very tradish, but very delish! I enjoy the mouthfeel the olive oil brings to the mix; it makes the topping richer and smoother. That said, feel free to omit it.*

• *While I like my fried food straight out of the oil, piping hot, these baked little nuggets are best when they come to room temperature, and even better as leftovers, straight out of the fridge.*

Arayes-Inspired Tacos

Serves 4 to 6 | Prep Time: 20 minutes | Cook Time: 15 minutes | Total Time: 35 minutes

Arayes are juicy meat-stuffed pita pockets that are a widely popular Middle Eastern street food. Some countries use a thin crisp pita, some use a fluffy thick pita, but either one gets stuffed with a deliciously spiced ground meat. The meat goes in raw and gets cooked in the pita, while the bread absorbs all those meaty juices and crisps up on the outside.

These super-easy-to-make tacos are inspired by that dish, swapping store-bought flour tortillas for the pita. Serve with a tangy and bitter tahini sauce that cuts through that meaty richness and a bright, refreshing chimichurri. This will be one of the quickest dinners you'll make, perfect for feeding a hungry crowd.

Tacos

1 pound ground lamb or ground beef (80/20)

½ cup chopped fresh parsley

4 garlic cloves, grated

1 tablespoon tomato paste

1 tablespoon onion powder

2 teaspoons ground cumin

1 teaspoon sweet paprika

¼ teaspoon cayenne pepper, plus more for serving

Kosher salt and black pepper

12 small (4½-inch) flour tortillas

Tahini Sauce

¼ cup tahini

¼ cup cold water

1 tablespoon fresh lemon juice

Kosher salt

Chimichurri Sauce

1½ cups chopped fresh parsley

½ cup extra-virgin olive oil, plus more as needed

2 teaspoons grated lime zest

⅓ cup fresh lime juice or red wine vinegar, plus more to taste

4 jalapeños, finely chopped

4 garlic cloves, finely grated

Kosher salt

Preheat the oven to 425°F. Line two baking sheets with parchment paper, and place an ovenproof wire rack (see Note) on each.

Make the tacos: In a medium bowl, combine the ground lamb, parsley, garlic, tomato paste, onion powder, cumin, paprika, cayenne, a big pinch of salt, and some black pepper. Use your hands or a silicone spatula to mix gently until combined. Divide the mixture into 12 equal portions.

Place a portion of the lamb mixture on a tortilla and use an offset spatula, spoon, or your hand to spread the mixture in an even layer all over the tortilla surface. Place the tortilla meat-side up on one of the wire racks. Repeat with the remaining tortillas and lamb mixture, placing them in rows on the racks. (A little overlap here is okay.)

Bake until the meat is browned all the way through, 12 to 14 minutes.

Preheat the broiler. Place the oven rack about 4 inches from the heating element. Broil until the meat is slightly crispy on top and the edges of the tortillas are charred, 2 to 3 minutes. Set aside to cool slightly.

Make the tahini sauce: In a medium bowl, whisk together the tahini, cold water, lemon juice, and a pinch of salt until smooth. The mixture will look clumpy and separated at first, but keep whisking and you'll get to a silky sauce. Taste and adjust the seasoning, adding more salt or lemon juice as needed.

Make the chimichurri: In a medium bowl, stir together the parsley, oil, lime zest, lime juice, jalapeños, garlic, and a pinch of salt. Taste and adjust the seasoning, adding more salt or lime juice as needed. To loosen the sauce, add another tablespoon or two of oil as desired.

To serve, drizzle the tacos with the tahini and top with a dollop of the chimichurri and a pinch of cayenne. Serve right away.

Note: *If you don't have ovenproof wire racks, you can also cook these in a cast-iron skillet over medium heat, starting with the meat side down, cooking until browned. Flip and cook until the tortilla is crisp. This takes a little more time but is just as tasty.*

Seared Steak
with Herby Zhug-Marinated Tomatoes

Serves 2 | Prep Time: 15 minutes, plus 30 minutes chilling | Cook Time: 10 minutes | Total Time: 55 minutes

While intimidating at first, a steak is one of the easiest things you'll learn to cook in your home kitchen, and it makes a decadent, yet quick and simple, dinner. You don't have to go all out and splurge on a bone-in rib eye on a random Tuesday night; save it for a special occasion. You can still try this recipe with a thinner rib eye or other preferred cuts. I like to pair my medium-rare steak with zhug—a spicy green Yemenite sauce packed with fresh herbs and spices—that I serve on top of the steak and use to marinate the tomatoes too.

Steak

1½ pounds bone-in rib eye (1 large or 2 small steaks), about 1 inch thick

Kosher salt

Zhug-Marinated Tomatoes

Seeds of 4 green cardamom pods

1 teaspoon coriander seeds

½ teaspoon cumin seeds

1 cup roughly chopped fresh cilantro

½ cup roughly chopped fresh parsley

⅓ cup extra-virgin olive oil, plus more as needed

2 small jalapeños, roughly chopped

3 garlic cloves, peeled but whole

3 tablespoons fresh lemon juice, plus more as needed

Kosher salt

1½ pounds beefsteak or heirloom tomatoes, sliced about ½ inch thick

Neutral oil, such as sunflower or grapeseed

Flaky salt, for serving

Prepare the steak: Place the steak on a piece of parchment paper and season generously on all sides with kosher salt. Set aside at room temperature for at least 30 minutes; up to 1 hour.

Make the zhug-marinated tomatoes: In a mortar and pestle, combine the cardamom seeds, coriander seeds, and cumin seeds. Crush them roughly, but no need to make a powder. (You can also do this by putting the spices between layers of paper towel and going over them a few times with a rolling pin.)

Transfer the crushed spices to a small dry skillet over medium heat and toast, shaking the pan occasionally, until slightly smoky and fragrant, about 2 minutes. Remove the pan from the heat.

Transfer the toasted spices to a food processor and add the cilantro, parsley, oil, jalapeños, garlic, lemon juice, and a pinch of kosher salt. Pulse until the zhug reaches a chunky, loose consistency. Taste and adjust the seasoning, adding more salt, lemon juice, or oil as needed.

In a medium bowl, add the sliced tomatoes and about ⅓ cup of the zhug and gently toss to coat. Set aside to marinate while you cook the steak. Reserve the rest of the zhug for serving.

Pat the steak dry with paper towels. Season on all sides with kosher salt (not as much as you used the first time, just a regular pinch).

Heat a large cast-iron skillet over medium heat until it starts smoking, about 5 minutes. Add about 1 tablespoon of neutral oil and swirl to coat the bottom. Carefully lay the steak in the pan, laying it down away from you to keep the oil from splashing in your direction. If you have a grill press or a smaller skillet, set it on the steak to weight it down and increase contact with the hot surface. Cook, undisturbed, until the underside takes on a beautifully caramelized crust, 5 to 6 minutes.

Use tongs to carefully flip the steak and cook for another 4 to 5 minutes. The perfect medium-rare steak will measure 120°F at its thickest point; cook the steak to your desired temperature. Transfer the steak to a plate, and let it rest for 8 to 10 minutes.

Slice the steak against the grain. Top with flaky salt and dollops of zhug, and serve with the tomato salad.

Honey Chipotle Salmon Tacos Dorados

Serves 4 | Prep Time: 35 minutes | Cook Time: 20 minutes | Total Time: 55 minutes

Rough day? I'm getting tacos dorados from my favorite local Mexican place. Hit an important milestone? I'm getting tacos dorados. Casual lunch? Tacos dorados. No food in the fridge? Ordering tacos dorados.

My favorite Mexican restaurant in town serves these crunchy fried corn tortillas stuffed with plain shredded chicken, topped with a massive amount of lettuce, radishes, avocados, and jalapeños. They're crisp, crunchy, refreshing, and so awkward to eat due to the number of toppings they're covered in—which is probably my favorite part.

I wanted to re-create a not-very-traditional version of my favorite takeout order, stuffing them with spiced chipotle salmon. Instead of deep-frying the tacos, I bake them to crispy perfection. Top with a ridiculous amount of crunchy veggies and drench in a chipotle sour cream and salty cheese.

Cucumber Radish Topping

8 to 10 small radishes, thinly sliced

3 Persian (mini) cucumbers, thinly sliced

1 small shallot, thinly sliced

1 medium jalapeño, thinly sliced

Kosher salt

Chipotle Sour Cream

1 cup sour cream

3 to 4 canned chipotle peppers in adobo sauce, finely chopped

2 garlic cloves, minced

Kosher salt

Salmon Tacos

1 pound skinless salmon fillets

4 to 6 canned chipotle peppers in adobo sauce, finely chopped

4 garlic cloves, minced

2 tablespoons honey

2 tablespoons all-purpose flour

1 tablespoon rice vinegar

2 teaspoons onion powder

1½ teaspoons ground cumin

Kosher salt

8 (6-inch) yellow corn tortillas

¼ cup neutral oil, such as sunflower or grapeseed, plus more as needed

Make the cucumber radish topping: In a medium bowl, toss together the radishes, cucumbers, shallot, jalapeño, and a big pinch of salt. Using your hands, massage the salt into the vegetables.

Make the chipotle sour cream: In a small bowl, stir together the sour cream, chipotles, garlic, and a pinch of salt. Refrigerate until ready to serve.

Make the salmon tacos: Preheat the oven to 425°F.

Cut the salmon fillets into ½-inch cubes. In a medium bowl, gently toss together the salmon, chipotles, garlic, honey, flour, vinegar, onion powder, cumin, and a big pinch of salt.

Arrange the tortillas on two baking sheets, letting them overlap a bit if needed. Warm the tortillas in the oven just until soft and pliable, 3 to 4 minutes. Stack the tortillas on a work surface and wrap the stack in a kitchen towel to stay soft. Leave the oven on.

Place a tortilla on the work surface and add about 2 tablespoons of the salmon mixture on half of the tortilla. Fold the tortilla in half to create a semicircle, pressing down gently to help the tortilla stick to the salmon mixture. Place the taco on a baking sheet. (If the tortilla unfolds, flip it on its other side.) Repeat with the remaining tortillas and salmon mixture. Using a pastry brush or your fingers, brush both sides of each taco with oil.

Return the tacos to the oven and bake until golden and crunchy, about 15 minutes. Flip the tacos and bake again until crispy on top, 3 to 4 minutes. Set the tortillas aside on a wire rack.

To finish: Drain the liquid from the bowl with the radishes and cucumbers. Add the lime zest and lime juice and stir to combine.

(recipe continues)

To Finish

Grated zest and juice of 1 lime
plus more for the lettuce

Thinly sliced crunchy lettuce

Kosher salt

Crumbled feta cheese (optional)

Salsa of choice (optional)

Lime wedges, for squeezing

To serve, arrange the tacos on a platter and top with the lettuce. Drizzle some lime juice on the lettuce, and a pinch of salt to season. Top with the cucumber radish mixture and dollops of the chipotle sour cream. If desired, sprinkle with feta and serve salsa on the side. Serve with lime wedges for squeezing.

Notes:

• If the number of items going into making these tacos feels overwhelming, a way to make things easier is to prep a few of these elements in advance. You can prepare the cucumber radish topping and chipotle sour cream and marinate the salmon cubes in advance. On the day of serving the tacos, all you'll have to do is assemble and cook them. Easy peasy!

• Speaking of cooking, if for whatever reason you can't bake them, you can also deep fry them in a hot oil bath or pan sear them like a quesadilla in a little bit of oil until the salmon mixture is cooked all the way through.

Potato Chip–Fried Fish Sandwiches
with Cilantro Lime Mayo

Serves 4 | Prep Time: 35 minutes | Cook Time: 10 minutes | Total Time: 45 minutes

This isn't just any ol' fried fish sandwich. First, the cod is seasoned with a fragrant homemade lime salt. We rub the salt and lime zest together to get the natural oils in the lime zest going and use it to season the finish. Second, I take the batter to the next level by tumbling the fish in crunchy potato chip crumbs before it gets fried up. (Yes, this fish is coated in potato chips!) It gets even better from there, with a creamy cilantro lime sauce and spicy slaw.

Cod Strips

Grated zest of 3 limes

2 teaspoons kosher salt

1 pound skinless cod fillets
(see Note)

Cilantro Lime Sauce

1½ cups packed fresh cilantro

4 scallions, chopped

Juice of 2 limes

Kosher salt

⅓ cup mayonnaise

Spicy Green Slaw

¼ small head green cabbage,
thinly sliced

2 medium jalapeños, thinly sliced

1 large shallot, thinly sliced

1 tablespoon sugar, plus more as
needed

Kosher salt

Juice of 1 lime

Crispy Cod

2 cups potato chips

¾ cup all-purpose flour

½ cup cornstarch

¼ teaspoon baking powder

Kosher salt

½ cup sparkling water or beer

Neutral oil, for shallow-frying

Assembly

4 ciabatta or potato rolls

Lime wedges, for squeezing

Prep the cod strips: In a small bowl, combine the lime zest and salt and use your fingertips to rub them together, releasing the lime oils into the salt. Slice the cod fillets into 2-inch-wide strips.

Set a rack over a baking sheet and place the cod strips on the rack. Season each strip generously with the lime salt.

Make the cilantro lime sauce: In a small food processor or blender, combine the cilantro, scallions, lime juice, a pinch of salt, and 1 tablespoon water. Process just until coarsely blended, adding more water as needed to help loosen the mixture.

Transfer the cilantro mixture to a medium bowl, add the mayonnaise, and whisk to combine. Set aside in a cool spot (see Note).

Make the spicy green slaw: In a medium bowl, combine the cabbage, jalapeños, shallot, sugar, and a hefty pinch of salt. Using clean hands, massage the mixture for 1 minute, helping the salt and sugar penetrate and soften the cabbage. Add the lime juice and a dollop of the creamy cilantro lime sauce and mix to combine.

Fry the crispy cod: Crush the chips right in the bag with your hands or a rolling pin. (Aim for a size similar to what you'd find at the bottom of the chip bag.) Spread the chip crumbs in a shallow bowl.

Add ½ cup of the flour in another shallow bowl. Coat a piece of fish in the flour and return it to the rack. Repeat with the remaining pieces of fish.

Notes:

- *The cilantro in the sauce will start oxidizing with time. This is totally fine! If you want to prevent that, blanch the herbs before blending or make the sauce right before serving.*

- *This recipe is very versatile when it comes to the type of fish you are using. If you aren't a big fan of cod or can't get your hands on any, salmon or trout will also work.*

(recipe continues)

In a medium bowl, whisk together the cornstarch, the remaining ¼ cup flour, the baking powder, and a good pinch of salt. Add the sparkling water and whisk again until smooth. The consistency of the batter should be like cream or buttermilk, so add a bit more flour or sparkling water as needed depending on your environment.

Set a rack over a baking sheet and place it near the stove. Pour 1 inch of neutral oil into a deep medium saucepan and heat over medium-high heat to 350°F.

Using a fork, dip a fish strip in the batter, shaking off any excess. Add the battered fish to the bowl of chip crumbs and roll it around to coat. Fry the fish until golden on the underside, 2 to 3 minutes. Flip and fry until the whole piece is crispy and golden. Use tongs or a slotted spoon to transfer the fried fish to the rack to drain and season immediately with a pinch of salt. Repeat with the remaining fish strips. Remove the pan from the heat.

Assemble the sandwiches: Spoon a bit of the cilantro lime sauce on the bottom half of each roll. Add one or two pieces of the crispy fish, followed by a dollop of the slaw and another spoonful of sauce. Add the top of the roll and serve right away with lime wedges on the side.

pasta-
palooza

Miso Mushroom Pasta

Serves 4 to 6 | Prep Time: 20 minutes | Cook Time: 40 minutes | Total Time: 1 hour

Are you searching for a hearty vegetarian pasta recipe? This miso mushroom pasta is what you're looking for. I bet it's no shock to you that miso paste is a staple in my fridge. The fermented soybean paste originating from Japan is rich, beautifully savory, subtly sweet, and pleasantly salty. Mushrooms are tossed together in butter and sizzled until deep brown in color with crispy edges. Throw in the pasta and scrape up any savory caramelized mushroom bits at the bottom of the pan with the help of some pasta water. Right before you're ready to serve, dollops of creamy miso are added to emulsify with the pasta water and coat the pasta just as an inviting silky cheese sauce would.

10 tablespoons (5 ounces) unsalted butter, plus more as needed

3 pounds mixed mushrooms, such as cremini, oyster, or shiitake, cut into ¼-inch slices

Kosher salt

1 pound pasta, any shape

9 garlic cloves, minced or finely grated

1 tablespoon red chile flakes, plus more for serving

Freshly ground black pepper

4 to 6 tablespoons white miso

Freshly grated Parmesan cheese, for serving (optional)

In a large pot, melt 6 tablespoons of the butter over medium-high heat. Add the mushrooms and toss to coat in the butter. This will seem like an impossible volume of mushrooms at first, but they cook down, I promise! Stirring occasionally, cook until the mushrooms have given up nearly all of their moisture, 20 to 25 minutes. If the pan looks dry, add another tablespoon of butter, and if the mushrooms seem to be browning too quickly or unevenly, feel free to reduce the heat.

Continue cooking until the mushrooms have taken on some color and crispy edges, stirring only once or twice, about another 10 minutes.

Meanwhile, bring a large pot of lightly salted water to a boil over medium-high heat. (We'll salt this pasta water a little less since the miso will add a good bit of salt later.) Add the pasta and cook, stirring occasionally, for 3 minutes less than what the package calls for. Remove the pan from the heat. Scoop out about 2 cups of pasta water and set aside.

To the mushrooms, add the remaining 4 tablespoons butter, the garlic, chile flakes, a pinch of salt, and a few grinds of black pepper. Cook, stirring, until fragrant, about 2 minutes.

Using tongs or a slotted spoon, add the cooked pasta and the reserved pasta water to the mushroom mixture, scraping up any browned bits at the bottom of the pan with a wooden spoon. Toss to combine and simmer until the pasta is tender, 2 to 3 minutes. Remove the pan from the heat.

Add 4 tablespoons of the miso and toss well to incorporate it into the sauce. Taste and add more miso as desired (see Note).

Divide among bowls and top with more chile flakes. If desired, sprinkle with grated Parmesan.

Note: *You'll notice the miso paste measurement in the ingredients isn't precise. That's because not all miso pastes are the same: some will be extra salty, some milder, lower in sodium. I encourage you to get to know your miso paste and feel your way through measuring it.*

Super-Simple Spicy Tomato Pasta

Serves 4 to 6 | Prep Time: 10 minutes | Cook Time: 40 minutes | Total Time: 50 minutes

While I can appreciate the convenience of a store-bought jar of tomato sauce, there's something about the smell of freshly made pasta sauce flooding your kitchen and inviting everyone to the table. This tomato sauce is one of the easiest pasta sauces you'll learn to make: If you can dump a bunch of tomatoes in a pot and wait for them to simmer a little bit, you're qualified for the job. Make this during peak tomato season or cook it up in the middle of January—either way it's a comforting, savory, and highly satisfying meal.

½ cup extra-virgin olive oil, plus more for drizzling

10 garlic cloves, thinly sliced

6 jarred Calabrian chiles, finely chopped, or 2 tablespoons Calabrian chile paste (see Note)

3 tablespoons Calabrian chile oil (optional)

1½ teaspoons coarsely ground black pepper

3 pounds cherry tomatoes or 1 (14.5-ounce) can plus 1 (28-ounce) can whole peeled tomatoes

3 sprigs fresh rosemary (optional)

Kosher salt

1 pound pasta, any shape

Freshly grated Parmesan cheese, for serving (optional)

In a large pot, heat the olive oil over medium heat. Add the garlic, Calabrian chiles, Calabrian chile oil (if using), and black pepper and cook just until fragrant, about 2 minutes. Add the tomatoes (with all the juices if using canned), rosemary sprigs (if using), and a big pinch of salt and stir to coat the tomatoes in the spicy oil. Bring to a simmer and reduce the heat to medium-low. Cook, stirring occasionally, letting the tomatoes slowly cook down into a loose sauce, breaking the tomatoes as you mix, 25 to 30 minutes.

Meanwhile, bring a large pot of well-salted water to a boil over medium-high heat. Add the pasta and cook for 3 minutes less than what the package calls for so that the pasta stays a little undercooked. Remove the pot from the heat. Scoop out about 2 cups of pasta water and set aside.

Reduce the heat under the tomato sauce to low and discard the rosemary sprigs (if used). Using tongs or a slotted spoon, transfer the pasta straight from the cooking water into the sauce and add about 1 cup of the reserved pasta water. Stir constantly until the sauce coats the pasta with a glossy consistency, 3 to 4 minutes, adding more pasta water as needed.

Divide the pasta among bowls and drizzle with some olive oil. If you'd like, sprinkle with Parmesan.

Note: *Calabrian chiles in oil will elevate this tomato sauce to a whole other level, but if you can't get your hands on a jar, you can absolutely use dried red chile flakes or a fresh hot red chile pepper instead.*

Butter Noodles
with Melting Onions and Cabbage

Serves 4 to 6 | Prep Time: 20 minutes | Cook Time: 40 minutes | Total Time: 1 hour

I like to describe this dish as the Eastern European butter noodle. It's the dish you make when the thought of dinner just seems too overwhelming. This would be one of those dishes children especially would look forward to; it's so simple, but it brings you straight back to childhood with every single bite. The cabbage and onions are slowly cooked until melted and sweet, then tossed with tender egg noodles and a hearty crack of black pepper for a mild kick. The extra dollop of softened butter in each serving bowl is a must: Mixing the butter with the noodles and watching it emulsify into a glossy, silky sauce was my favorite part growing up.

⅓ cup neutral oil, such as sunflower or grapeseed, plus more as needed

1½ tablespoons coarsely cracked black peppercorns, plus more for serving

3 medium yellow onions, sliced ¼ inch thick

Kosher salt

3-pound head green cabbage, cut into ¼-inch-wide slices

1 pound egg noodles, or pasta such as tagliatelle or pappardelle

8 to 12 tablespoons salted butter, at room temperature, for serving

In a large pot, heat the oil over medium heat. Add the cracked pepper and fry until fragrant, about 1 minute. Add the onion and a pinch of salt and cook, stirring occasionally, until translucent, 6 to 8 minutes. Add the cabbage and continue cooking, stirring frequently, until the cabbage and onion are both a deep golden brown and there's a golden-brown crust forming at the bottom of the pot, 25 to 30 minutes. If the pot looks dry, add another tablespoon or so of oil to help the cabbage fry and caramelize.

While the cabbage cooks, bring a large pot of well-salted water to a boil over medium-high heat. Add the noodles and cook for 3 minutes less than what the package calls for, so they're a little undercooked. Remove the pot from the heat.

Using tongs or a slotted spoon, add the pasta directly to the cabbage and onion and stir to combine. Add about ½ cup of pasta water and scrape the bottom of the pan to release all the browned, flavorful bits from the bottom of the pan. Add more pasta water as needed to help create a thin but silky sauce that clings to the noodles. Taste and season with more salt as needed. Remove the pot from the heat.

Divide the noodles among bowls and top each bowl with 2 tablespoons of salted butter and more freshly cracked black pepper. Enjoy watching the butter melt in each bowl, stir until glossy and creamy.

Cheese-Stuffed Pasta Shells Doused
with Saucy Summer Veg

Serves 8 to 10 | Prep Time: 25 minutes | Cook Time: 1 hour 35 minutes | Total Time: 2 hours

Whenever I develop a recipe like this, I try my hardest to remove that additional step of precooking the pasta while adding an extra pot to your dirty dish pile. For this cheesy number, hard pasta shells are stuffed with an herby, peppery ricotta mixture, then nestled into the sauce. Covering the casserole allows the pasta to steam and absorb moisture while cooking in the oven.

For the base sauce, my biggest inspiration was ratatouille—the French vegetable dish, not the famous rat. I tried using vegetables typically found in a ratatouille to replicate a tomato-y, veggie sauce reminiscent of the French delicacy.

⅓ cup extra-virgin olive oil, plus more for drizzling

1 large yellow onion, chopped

1 medium eggplant, cut into ½-inch cubes

2 medium zucchini, cut into ½-inch cubes

Kosher salt

2 red bell peppers, chopped

1 (28-ounce) can whole peeled tomatoes

1 pound whole-milk ricotta cheese

2 tablespoons finely chopped fresh parsley

1 garlic clove, minced or finely grated

Freshly ground black pepper

22 to 25 jumbo pasta shells (about 6½ ounces)

12 ounces whole-milk low-moisture mozzarella cheese, coarsely grated

Torn fresh basil leaves, for serving

Preheat the oven to 400°F.

In a large saucepan, heat the oil over medium-high heat for 1 to 2 minutes. Add the onion and cook, stirring occasionally, until soft and translucent, 4 to 5 minutes. Add the eggplant, zucchini, and a big pinch of salt and cook, stirring occasionally, until the vegetables have cooked down and softened significantly, 10 to 12 minutes.

Add the bell peppers and cook, stirring occasionally, until softened, about 5 more minutes. Reduce the heat to medium and add the canned tomatoes, crushing the whole tomatoes with your hands as you add them. Stir to combine and season with another big pinch of salt. Cook, stirring frequently, until fragrant and saucy, 10 to 12 minutes. The sauce will have a loose, liquid consistency.

Remove the pan from the heat. In a 9 × 13-inch baking pan, carefully add the sauce.

In a medium bowl, combine the ricotta, parsley, garlic, a pinch of salt, and black pepper to taste. Stuff the dry shells with about 1 tablespoon of the ricotta mixture, scraping off any excess using your finger or a spatula. (You can also stuff the shells using a piping bag, piping the mixture straight in the shell.) Gently nestle each shell into the sauce and repeat with the remaining shells. If you end up with leftover ricotta mixture, dot the remainder between the shells.

Tightly cover the pan with foil and bake for 1 hour.

Carefully remove the foil and sprinkle the mozzarella all over the shells. Bake until the cheese has fully melted, 5 to 7 minutes. Preheat the broiler. Place the oven rack about 4 inches from the heating element. Broil just until the cheese is bubbling and slightly charred, 1 to 2 minutes.

Serve hot with freshly torn basil and a drizzle of olive oil.

Brie Mac and Cheese
with Crunchy Panko

Serves 4 to 6 | Prep Time: 10 minutes | Cook Time: 20 minutes | Total Time: 30 minutes

While I can appreciate a classic mac 'n' cheese casserole for the comforting, decadent dish that it is, I also acknowledge how fussy it can be to make. Depending on the recipe, you end up dirtying like twelve dishes, the whole thing can take a couple of hours from start to finish, and the béchamel may be tricky to keep an eye on. It's a lot! This 30-minute recipe gives you that same comforting, cheesy result with a fraction of the effort. We've still got a crunchy topping, flavored with crispy shallots and garlic, plus bites of pasta drenched in sauce. The melted Brie replaces the sometimes finicky béchamel, melting easily into a creamy base that's a perfect pairing with the sharp cheddar. It's a simple but effective way to have mac 'n' cheese any night of the week.

Garlicky Panko

4 tablespoons (2 ounces) unsalted butter

2 small shallots, finely chopped

4 garlic cloves, minced or finely grated

⅔ cup panko or other bread crumbs

Kosher salt

Brie Mac and Cheese

Kosher salt

1 pound short pasta, such as macaroni, shells, or rigatoni

10 ounces double-cream Brie cheese, rind removed, cheese cut into cubes

4 tablespoons (2 ounces) unsalted butter, cut into cubes

8 ounces sharp white cheddar or Gruyère cheese, finely grated

Make the garlicky panko: In a small skillet, melt the butter over medium heat. Add the shallots and cook, stirring frequently, until translucent and softened, 3 to 4 minutes. Add the garlic and cook until just fragrant, 1 to 2 minutes. Add the panko, a pinch of salt, and stir to coat. Reduce the heat to medium-low and cook, stirring constantly, until the panko is golden and crispy, 5 to 6 minutes. Remove the pan from the heat.

Make the Brie mac and cheese: Bring a large pot of well-salted water to a boil. Add the pasta and cook for 3 minutes less than what the package calls for. Remove the pan from the heat. Reserving 2 cups of the cooking water, drain the pasta and return it to the pot.

Add ½ cup of the reserved pasta water to the pasta along with the cubed Brie and butter. Stir vigorously, using the residual heat in the pan to melt the Brie and butter.

Return the pot to medium-low heat. Add another 1 cup of the pasta water, plus a handful of the shredded cheddar. Stir vigorously once again to help the cheese melt. Add the remaining cheddar in batches, stirring until completely emulsified into the sauce. Add a splash more pasta water to loosen the sauce if needed. Remove the pot from the heat.

Divide the pasta among bowls, top with the crispy panko, and serve.

Frizzled Shallot Carbonara

Serves 4 to 6 | Prep Time: 15 minutes | Cook Time: 25 minutes | Total Time: 40 minutes

This is not a classic carbonara. Instead of the traditional guanciale, this vegetarian recipe uses pantry-friendly shallot plus garlic, chile flakes, and black pepper for the creamy egg-based sauce. With a little bit of technique and patience, we can extract maximal flavor out of these humble ingredients. If you're second-guessing using eggs in your pasta sauce, don't worry—this is nothing like eating scrambled eggs with spaghetti. The yolks and cheese emulsify into a rich, creamy, silky sauce. Serve with more frizzly, garlicky caramelized shallot on top.

½ cup extra-virgin olive oil, plus more for drizzling

6 medium shallots, finely chopped

Kosher salt

10 garlic cloves, minced or finely grated

1 teaspoon black peppercorns, crushed

1 teaspoon red chile flakes

1 pound dried long pasta, such as spaghetti or linguine

9 large egg yolks

1½ cups (about 4½ ounces) packed finely grated Parmesan cheese, plus more for serving

In a large skillet, heat the oil over medium heat. Add the shallots and a pinch of salt and cook, stirring occasionally, until soft and translucent, 4 to 6 minutes. Reduce the heat to medium-low and continue cooking, stirring occasionally, until the shallots darken in color, 8 to 12 minutes. If you feel like the shallots are browning too fast, carefully add a splash of water to the pan, scrape up the browned bits on the bottom, and continue cooking.

Add the garlic, crushed peppercorns, and chile flakes and cook just until fragrant, about 1 minute. Remove the pan from the heat. Reserve about ¼ cup of the shallot mixture in a small bowl and set the bowl and the pan aside.

Meanwhile, bring a large pot of well-salted water to a boil over medium-high heat. Add the pasta and cook, stirring occasionally, for 3 minutes less than what the package calls for.

While the pasta cooks, in a medium bowl, whisk together the egg yolks and Parmesan. Use a heatproof measuring cup to scoop out about 1½ cups of the hot, starchy cooking water from the pasta. Whisking constantly, slowly stream the hot pasta water into the egg mixture to create a thin, saucy custard.

Return the pan with the shallots to medium heat and heat for a couple of minutes while the pasta finishes cooking.

Remove the pasta pot from the heat. Using a pair of tongs, transfer the pasta to the shallot mixture. Add ¾ cup of the pasta water to the mixture and toss well to combine. Reduce the heat to medium-low. Pour the egg yolk mixture all over the pasta and stir vigorously and continuously for 1 to 2 minutes, until the sauce thickens. If you find the sauce to be a bit too thick, add a splash of the pasta water to thin it out and stir again to emulsify. Remove the pan from the heat.

Divide the pasta among plates and top with the reserved shallot mixture, a shower of grated Parmesan, and a drizzle of olive oil. Serve immediately.

Many Mushrooms Lasagna

Serves 6 to 8 | Prep Time: 25 minutes | Cook Time: 1 hour 30 minutes | Total Time: 1 hour 55 minutes

If you're like me and the thought of boiling lasagna noodles, going through the fuss of keeping them from sticking to each other or perfectly layering them, stresses you out, so much so that you make lasagna only a couple times a year, this recipe is for you. I had but one mission developing this recipe: loosen up the rules and transform the typical lasagna-making process into a more approachable one. Break the dry noodles into smaller pieces, toss in a silky, mushroomy béchamel sauce, then layer the hard noodles with dollops of creamy ricotta, stretchy mozzarella, and perfectly cooked mushrooms. You'll be left with an impressive, highly comforting vegetarian centerpiece and significantly fewer dishes to clean.

8 tablespoons (4 ounces) unsalted butter

2 pounds mixed mushrooms, such as cremini, oyster, or shiitake, torn into chunks

5 garlic cloves, finely chopped

2 teaspoons coarsely cracked black pepper, plus more as needed

Kosher salt

3 tablespoons all-purpose flour

4 cups whole milk

2 sprigs fresh rosemary (optional)

8 ounces lasagna noodles (uncooked)

1½ cups whole-milk ricotta cheese

½ cup finely grated Parmesan cheese

1 pound whole-milk low-moisture mozzarella cheese, coarsely grated

In a large Dutch oven or other heavy pot, melt the butter over medium heat until sizzling. Add the mushrooms and cook, stirring frequently, until the mushrooms have cooked out their liquid and are deeply browned, about 30 minutes.

Reduce the heat to medium-low. Add the garlic, black pepper, and a big pinch of salt and cook until fragrant, 1 to 2 minutes. Add the flour and stir to coat the mushrooms. Stirring constantly, slowly add the milk. Add the rosemary (if using), bring to a simmer, and cook, stirring occasionally, until the sauce thickens, 4 to 6 minutes. The consistency should be similar to heavy cream. Taste and adjust the salt as needed.

Break the lasagna noodles into smaller pieces, 3 to 4 pieces per noodle, and add them to the simmering sauce. Toss the noodles in the sauce, remove the pan from the heat. Remove and discard the rosemary (if using).

In a medium bowl, combine the ricotta, Parmesan, a pinch of salt, and a few grinds of black pepper. Stir to combine.

Preheat the oven to 400°F.

In a 10-inch round pan or 9-inch square pan, spread a small dollop of the ricotta mixture on the bottom. Add about one-third of the saucy mushroom/noodle mixture and arrange it in an even-ish layer. (This isn't like traditional lasagna where you're trying to line the noodles up perfectly, so don't overthink it!) Add one-third of the ricotta mixture, spreading it gently into an even layer, and top with one-third of the mozzarella. Repeat with another third of the mushroom/noodle mixture, another third of the ricotta mixture, and another third of mozzarella. Repeat once more, but this time only with the remaining mushroom/noodle mixture and ricotta mixture, reserving the last bit of mozzarella for later. Your last layer should have the ricotta on top. Tightly cover the pan with foil.

Bake for 45 to 50 minutes. Remove the foil and sprinkle the reserved mozzarella on top of the lasagna. Preheat the broiler. Place the oven rack about 4 inches from the heating element. Broil until the mozzarella is melted, bubbling, and a bit browned, 3 to 5 minutes.

Let cool for 5 minutes before serving.

Creamy Roasted Red Pepper Pasta

Serves 4 to 6 | Prep Time: 15 minutes | Cook Time: 20 minutes | Total Time: 35 minutes

A majority of my recipes are born of a need to clean old ingredients out of my pantry. One time, something came over me in the clearance aisle of a supermarket and I bought a dozen jars of roasted red peppers for less than $1—great deal. After tossing them in salads, salsas, soups, and pizzas, my list of things-to-throw-roasted-peppers-in started to feel a little limited. Until I added a bunch of them to a creamy pasta sauce and the result was outstanding: spicy, savory, a little sweet, perfectly creamy.

If you're a fan of pasta alla vodka, this recipe should be up your alley. It's like its cousin, with more personal style. The roasted red pepper brings a mild sweetness, more body, and a palatable savoriness to the sauce, with a rich orange color ready to stain your white shirt after a hungry slurp.

Kosher salt

1 pound pasta of choice, such as rigatoni, shells, spaghetti

½ cup extra-virgin olive oil, plus more for drizzling

2 medium shallots, roughly chopped

2 tablespoons tomato paste

6 garlic cloves, roughly chopped

2 teaspoons coarsely cracked black pepper

½ teaspoon red chile flakes, or more to taste

½ teaspoon cayenne pepper

2 (16-ounce) jars roasted red peppers, drained

1½ cups (about 4½ ounces) finely grated Parmesan cheese, plus more for serving

1 cup chopped fresh basil leaves

Bring a large pot of well-salted water to a boil over medium-high heat. Add the pasta and cook for 3 minutes less than what the package calls for. Reserving 3 cups of the pasta water, drain the pasta.

In a large pot, heat the oil over medium heat. Add the shallots and cook, stirring occasionally, until translucent and softened, about 4 minutes. Add the tomato paste, garlic, black pepper, chile flakes, and cayenne and cook, stirring, until fragrant, 2 to 3 minutes. Add the roasted peppers, mix with the spices and oil, and cook until the peppers color the oil and are warmed through, about 3 minutes. Remove the pan from the heat.

Carefully transfer the pepper mixture to a blender or food processor. Add the Parmesan, 1 cup of the pasta water, and the basil. Remove the center plug in the blender lid to let steam vent out, and blend until very smooth.

Return the sauce to the pot and set over medium heat. Add the drained pasta and another splash of the pasta water. Simmer, stirring and tossing the pasta in the sauce, until the pasta is cooked all the way through and the sauce is silky, 3 to 5 minutes. Loosen the sauce with a bit more pasta water as needed and taste, adjusting the salt as needed.

Divide the pasta among bowls and top with additional Parmesan and a drizzle of extra-virgin olive oil.

Brown Butter Caramelized Zucchini Pasta

Serves 4 to 6 | Prep Time: 30 minutes | Cook Time: 40 minutes | Total Time: 1 hour 10 minutes

In every single place I've ever lived, I've had a neighbor who would bless me with their zucchini or summer squash harvest every single summer. "Bless" might be a stretch. It's a blessing for the first couple of giant homegrown squashes. Then your smile fades away while you panic about what else you could possibly make with those three ridiculously gigantic zucchini staring at you from the corner of your kitchen.

This! This is the recipe you make. This recipe takes an exorbitant amount of squash and cooks it down to a deeply flavorful base, perfect for a pasta sauce.

6 pounds zucchini (about 10 medium)

⅓ cup kosher salt, plus more as needed

10 tablespoons (5 ounces) unsalted butter

4 garlic cloves, thinly sliced

1 tablespoon grated lemon zest (from 2 small lemons)

Freshly ground black pepper

1 pound dried long pasta

For Serving

Grated Parmesan cheese

Fresh basil leaves

Extra-virgin olive oil, for drizzling

Trim the stem ends of the zucchini. Using a mandoline or a sharp knife, slice the zucchini crosswise into ⅛-inch-thick coins. Add the sliced zucchini to a large bowl. Add the salt and roughly massage it into the zucchini for 3 to 4 minutes by squeezing the zucchini in your hands (some of the zucchini will tear, it's totally fine!). The salt helps draw out the moisture and soften the zucchini. Set the zucchini aside for 10 minutes.

Place a colander over a large bowl. Pour the zucchini into the colander. The bowl will get filled with about 3 cups of liquid. Working in batches, vigorously squeeze handfuls of zucchini over the bowl to remove any excess moisture. You should be able to extract an additional 1 to 2 cups of liquid. Reserve the drained zucchini juice.

In a large pot, melt 6 tablespoons of the butter over medium-high heat. Add about one-third of the zucchini to the skillet. Press it down in an even layer using a silicone spatula. Fry the zucchini for 9 to 12 minutes, mostly undisturbed, mixing every 3 to 4 minutes, or whenever the zucchini develops golden brown spots and crispy edges. Reduce the heat as needed to prevent the zucchini from burning. Using a slotted spoon, transfer the golden, soft, caramelized zucchini to a medium bowl.

Repeat with the remaining two batches of zucchini, adding 2 tablespoons of butter to the pot before cooking each batch.

Return the caramelized zucchini to the pot over medium heat. Add the garlic, lemon zest, and black pepper to taste. Cook, stirring, until the garlic and lemon are fragrant, about 2 minutes. Remove the pot from the heat.

Meanwhile, to a large pot, add the reserved salty zucchini juice and enough water to cook the pasta in. Bring to a boil. Add the pasta and cook for about 3 minutes less than what the package calls for.

Return the pot with the zucchini to medium heat. Use tongs to transfer the undercooked pasta straight from the boiling water to the zucchini, and add about 1 cup of the pasta water. Toss well with tongs to coat the pasta with the zucchini, adding more pasta water as needed to loosen up the mixture. Taste and season with salt as needed.

To serve: Top with grated Parmesan, basil, and a drizzle of olive oil.

Caramelized Lemon Pesto Pasta

Serves 4 to 6 | Prep Time: 25 minutes | Cook Time: 25 minutes | Total Time: 50 minutes

Another page, another caramelized lemon recipe! This isn't the first time you're seeing this ingredient in the book. I like it so much I made it my mission to demonstrate its versatility, whether I'm showcasing it in a sauce, over fried chicken (see Chicken Schnitzel, page 81), or in a salad dressing (see Crisp Green Salad with Caramelized Citrus Dressing, page 205). This lemon pesto started as a completely different recipe that ended up not working out. I decided to blend the forever-present caramelized lemons from my fridge into a pesto-like mixture. While this "pesto" might be missing the basil, you certainly won't miss out on any flavor. The lemon paste emulsifies with the starchy pasta water into a decadent sauce, ready to coat your favorite pasta shape. It's unique, yet familiar at the same time—my favorite combination.

1½ cups chopped walnuts

¾ cup extra-virgin olive oil, plus more for cooking the lemons

3 medium Meyer or regular lemons (see page 21), very thinly sliced (⅛ to ¼ inch), seeded, ends reserved

1½ cups (about 4½ ounces) finely grated Parmesan cheese, plus more for serving

3 garlic cloves

Kosher salt

1 pound pasta, any shape

In a large skillet, toast the walnuts over medium heat, shaking the pan occasionally, until fragrant and toasty, 3 to 4 minutes. Remove the pan from the heat. Transfer the walnuts to a food processor. Carefully wipe the pan clean.

Return the pan to medium heat and add about 2 tablespoons of the olive oil. Working in batches, arrange the lemon slices in an even layer in the pan. Cook the lemon slices, undisturbed, until they begin to caramelize and take on a darker color around the pith and peel, 2 to 3 minutes. Flip the slices and cook until most of the center flesh has cooked away and the lemons are caramelized, 2 to 3 minutes. Set aside a few fried lemon slices for serving and transfer the remaining slices and any residual oil to the food processor. Use the reserved lemon ends to clean the pan between batches, and scrape off any solids into the food processor, then discard the ends. This will ensure there are no lemon bits in the pan that will burn as you cook an additional batch of lemons. Repeat with any remaining lemon slices, adding 2 tablespoons of oil to the pan.

To the food processor, add the Parmesan, garlic, ¾ cup olive oil, and a hefty pinch of salt. Pulse until just combined, aiming for a coarse paste. Taste and add more salt or olive oil as needed.

Meanwhile, bring a large pot of well-salted water to a boil over medium-high heat. Add the pasta and cook for a minute less than what the package directions call for. Reserving 2 cups of the pasta water, drain the pasta and return it to the pot.

Set the pot of pasta over low heat and add the pesto and about 1 cup of the pasta water. Mix to coat the pasta in the pesto, adding more pasta water a splash at a time to bring it to a saucy, glossy consistency.

Divide the pasta among bowls, top with the reserved lemon slices and a shower of Parmesan, and serve immediately.

15-Minute Double-Garlic Pasta

Serves 4 to 6 | Prep Time: 5 minutes | Cook Time: 10 minutes | Total Time: 15 minutes

I love aglio e olio pasta—it's so simple and it hits all the right spots every single time. But you know what? I wish it had even more garlic flavor! Once you sizzle the garlic in oil, it loses most of its sharp flavor, so in this recipe we're doubling up. You get all the savor of a classic aglio e olio but kicked up. Not only will we sauté the garlic to infuse the olive oil for the sauce, we're adding fresh garlic cloves straight into the pasta as soon as it comes off the stove. The residual heat will cook them just enough to take the edge off, leaving you with the punchy garlic flavor I can't get enough of.

Kosher salt

1 pound pasta, any shape

⅓ cup extra-virgin olive oil, plus more for drizzling

10 garlic cloves, thinly sliced, plus 8 garlic cloves, minced or finely grated

½ cup finely chopped fresh parsley

2 fresh red Fresno chiles, finely chopped

1½ teaspoons Aleppo pepper or red chile flakes

8 tablespoons (4 ounces) unsalted butter, cut into 1-tablespoon chunks

Grated Parmesan cheese, for serving (optional)

Bring a large pot of well-salted water to a boil over medium-high heat. Add the pasta and cook for 3 minutes less than what the package calls for. Remove the pan from the heat.

Meanwhile, in a large skillet, combine the oil, 10 thinly sliced garlic cloves, about two-thirds of the parsley, the Fresno chiles, and Aleppo pepper. Set the pan over medium heat and cook just until fragrant, 2 to 3 minutes.

Using tongs or a slotted spoon, add the cooked pasta to the pan, plus 1 cup of the pasta water. Stir and toss to emulsify the starchy pasta water and oil into a thin, silky sauce. Add more pasta water as needed and simmer the pasta until cooked through, another minute or two. Remove the pan from the heat.

Add the butter, the remaining parsley, and the remaining 8 grated or minced garlic cloves, and stir until the butter is melted and fully incorporated. Taste and season with more salt as needed.

Divide the pasta among bowls and top with Parmesan (if using) and a drizzle of olive oil. Serve right away.

veg
out

Comforting Mushroom Stew
with Creamy Polenta

Serves 4 | Prep Time: 20 minutes | Cook Time: 1 hour 25 minutes | Total Time: 1 hour 45 minutes

Growing up, my cousins and I would go with our mothers to forage for golden chanterelles up in the hills of our hometown: My aunt would identify them, my mother would carry the box, while their little ones played catch in the forest. Funny enough, back then we didn't consider them luxurious. We'd come home and get straight to work. The children would brush the dirt off all the mushrooms while my aunt sautéed coarsely chopped veggies as the base of the stew. She'd toss in the freshly torn golden chanterelles and finish the stew with a very memorable shower of fresh parsley.

   While I'm not going to have you go foraging for chanterelles, nor make you spend a lot of money for the number you'd need to make this recipe, I'll encourage you to use a variety of store-bought mushrooms for a more complex flavor.

Mushroom Stew

6 tablespoons extra-virgin olive oil

1½ to 2 pounds mixed mushrooms, torn into big chunks

Kosher salt

2 medium shallots, chopped

4 garlic cloves, chopped

1½ teaspoons cumin seeds

½ teaspoon black pepper

¼ teaspoon red chile flakes

2 tablespoons soy sauce

1 tablespoon rice vinegar

2 tablespoons cornstarch

¼ cup chopped fresh parsley

Creamy Polenta

Kosher salt

1 cup fine polenta

½ cup heavy cream

½ cup finely grated Parmesan cheese

4 tablespoons (2 ounces) unsalted butter

For Serving

Extra-virgin olive oil, for drizzling

Grated Parmesan cheese

Chopped fresh parsley

Make the mushroom stew: In a large, deep skillet, heat 4 tablespoons of the oil over medium-high heat. Add the mushrooms and a big pinch of salt and cook, stirring frequently, until golden and beginning to crisp along the edges, 20 to 30 minutes. Transfer the mushrooms to a plate.

Reduce the heat to medium and heat the remaining 2 tablespoons oil and the shallots and cook, stirring occasionally, until soft and translucent, about 4 minutes. Add the garlic, cumin seeds, black pepper, and chile flakes and cook until fragrant, 1 to 2 minutes. Add the soy sauce and vinegar and scrape up any browned bits from the bottom of the pan with a wooden spoon.

Return the mushrooms to the pan and add the cornstarch, tossing until the mushrooms are evenly coated. While stirring constantly, slowly add 2 cups water. Bring to a boil. Reduce the heat to medium-low and simmer, stirring occasionally, until the stew thickens, 10 to 15 minutes. Taste and adjust the seasoning, adding more salt or chile flakes as needed. Remove the pan from the heat and stir in the parsley.

Make the polenta: In a medium saucepan, bring 4 cups water to a boil over medium heat. Season the water with a big pinch of salt. Constantly whisk as you add the polenta. Reduce the heat to medium-low and simmer the polenta, whisking about every minute or so, until each grain is tender and the consistency is similar to mashed potatoes or a thick porridge, 15 to 20 minutes. If the polenta gets too hard to whisk, switch to a wooden spoon.

Stir in the cream and Parmesan and continue cooking and stirring for 8 to 10 minutes. Taste and check the polenta: If it's grainy, it needs more time; if it's creamy and each grain is tender all the way through, it's ready. Remove the pan from the heat. Add the butter and stir until it's fully melted. Taste and season with more salt as needed.

To serve: Add a big dollop of polenta to a plate and create a well in the middle. Spoon the mushroom stew onto the polenta and top with a drizzle of olive oil, plus more cheese and a sprinkle of fresh parsley.

Saucy Beans al Limone

Serves 2 to 4 | Prep Time: 5 minutes | Cook Time: 15 minutes | Total Time: 20 minutes

Think pasta al limone, but beans: butter beans tossed in a bright, lemony sauce. And I've said it before and I'll say it again: Butter beans outshine most beans. They hold their shape, have a sturdy texture, and can hold on to any sauce you toss them in. They're like little dumplings, ready to absorb your toppings.

I love making this and doubling the batch so I can enjoy leftovers for lunch, dinner, or even breakfast. It's one of those quick recipes that seems like you've put in a ton of effort when it really took only 15 minutes. Top it with a silky soft-boiled egg if you like! The creamy yolk coats the beans, mixes with the sauce, and all you'll need is crusty bread for dipping.

2 to 4 large eggs (optional)

2 (15-ounce) cans butter beans or lima beans, drained and rinsed (see Note)

2 teaspoons grated lemon zest (about 1 small lemon)

½ cup fresh lemon juice (about 1½ lemons)

Kosher salt

¼ cup finely grated Parmesan cheese

3 tablespoons unsalted butter

For Serving

Finely grated Parmesan cheese

Grated lemon zest

Red chile flakes (optional)

Extra-virgin olive oil

Flaky salt

Crusty bread

If using the eggs, fill a medium bowl with ice water. Bring a small saucepan of water to a boil over medium-high heat. Using a spoon, gently lower in the eggs. For a runny yolk, boil for 6 minutes; for a jammy yolk, boil for 7 to 8 minutes; for hard yolks, boil for 10 to 12 minutes. Remove the pan from the heat and immediately transfer the eggs to the ice bath.

In a medium saucepan, combine the beans, lemon zest, lemon juice, and a pinch of kosher salt. Cook over medium heat, stirring frequently, until the lemon juice has reduced and the beans look saucy, 6 to 8 minutes.

Reduce the heat to medium-low and add the Parmesan and butter. Using a wooden spoon, vigorously mix the cheese and butter into the beans while shaking the saucepan back and forth. This constant motion will help emulsify the cheese and butter and create a silky sauce. Add a tablespoon of water to thin out the sauce as needed.

To serve: Divide the saucy beans into bowls and top with more grated Parmesan, lemon zest, and chile flakes (if you like), plus a good glug of olive oil. Peel the boiled eggs and place them on top, slicing them open to release the luscious yolk all over the beans. Top with flaky salt and serve right away with crusty bread.

Note: *If you can't get your hands on butter (or lima) beans, garbanzo or Great Northern beans will work just as well.*

Cozy Veggie Pot Pie

Serves 6 to 8 | Prep Time: 30 minutes | Cook Time: 50 minutes | Total Time: 1 hour 20 minutes

Nothing screams comfort food like some sort of saucy, hearty stew covered in a buttery, flaky puff pastry. The best part is this delicious pot pie is the epitome of a clean-out-the-fridge type of dish. Don't be afraid to make it your own. Play around with spices and use those veggie scraps!

The leftovers are amazing with a fried egg on top for breakfast. I like to reheat it in my toaster oven while my egg is frying.

Filling

¼ cup extra-virgin olive oil

1 medium yellow onion, chopped

Kosher salt

3 celery stalks, chopped

3 medium carrots, chopped

1 medium red bell pepper, chopped

2 tablespoons chopped fresh rosemary

4 garlic cloves, chopped

1½ teaspoons sweet paprika

½ teaspoon ground cumin

¼ teaspoon cayenne pepper

2 (15-ounce) cans brown lentils, drained and rinsed

2 tablespoons cornstarch

1 cup whole milk or unsweetened nondairy milk

¼ cup chopped fresh parsley, plus more for serving

Pastry

1 large egg or 1 tablespoon unsweetened nondairy milk, for brushing

All-purpose flour, for dusting

½ pound frozen puff pastry, thawed overnight in the fridge

Preheat the oven to 400°F.

Make the filling: In a large Dutch oven or heavy-bottomed pot, heat the oil over medium heat. Add the onion and a big pinch of salt and cook, stirring occasionally, until the onion is soft and translucent, 4 to 5 minutes. Add the celery and carrots and cook, stirring, until the carrots are softened slightly, 6 to 8 minutes. Add the red bell pepper and rosemary and cook, stirring, until the pepper is softened, 3 to 4 minutes. Add the garlic, paprika, cumin, and cayenne and cook, stirring frequently, until fragrant, 1 to 2 minutes. Stir in the lentils.

Add the cornstarch and use a wooden spoon to toss and coat the vegetables. Stirring constantly, add 1 cup water, followed by the milk. Cook, stirring occasionally, until visibly thickened, 4 to 5 minutes. Remove the pot from the heat and stir in the parsley. Taste and adjust the salt as needed.

Carefully transfer the mixture to a 9- to 10-inch cast-iron skillet or a deep casserole dish.

Prepare the pastry: In a small bowl, whisk together the egg and 1 tablespoon water to make an egg wash. If using nondairy milk, simply add it to a small bowl.

Dust a work surface with flour. Working quickly to keep the pastry cold, roll it out into a sheet ¼ inch thick. Use a glass or round cookie cutter to cut out as many rounds as you can in the dough. Place the dough rounds in an even layer on top of the vegetable filling, avoiding overlap as much as you can (a little is okay). Lightly brush the pastry rounds with the egg wash or nondairy milk.

Bake until the pastry is puffed up, golden, and firm, about 25 minutes. Let cool 5 minutes before serving.

Divide the pot pie among plates or bowls, top with more fresh parsley, and serve.

Note: *This recipe uses celery, carrots, and bell pepper, but you can make this pie out of any veg looking rough or going mushy in your kitchen. I'm talking broccoli stalks, half a cabbage, dry cauliflower florets, and old zucchini—all good.*

Mushroom Shawarma

Serves 4 | Prep Time: 45 minutes | Cook Time: 40 minutes | Total Time: 1 hour 25 minutes

A meatless recipe guaranteed to satisfy any hungry bellies, this mushroom shawarma is the perfect vegetarian alternative to the popular meat-based street food. Season with rich, smoky flavors and the mushrooms will absorb them like a sponge. Sandwich them in an airy pita with fresh salad and dollop garlicky yogurt, and enjoy.

Spiced Roasted Mushrooms

6 tablespoons extra-virgin olive oil

4 garlic cloves, grated

½ tablespoon tomato paste

1 tablespoon Dijon mustard

1 tablespoon sugar

1½ teaspoons ground cumin

1 teaspoon sweet paprika

½ teaspoon ground cinnamon

Kosher salt

1½ pounds mixed mushrooms, such as oyster or cremini, torn into bite-size pieces

3 medium shallots, sliced

Shirazi Salad

2 medium Roma tomatoes, diced

2 Persian (mini) cucumbers, diced

1 small shallot, finely chopped

¼ cup chopped fresh parsley

2 tablespoons extra-virgin olive oil

1 tablespoon rice vinegar or fresh lemon juice

Kosher salt

Garlicky Yogurt

1 cup whole-milk Greek yogurt

¼ cup finely chopped fresh dill

2 garlic cloves, minced

1 tablespoon rice vinegar or fresh lemon juice

Kosher salt

4 to 8 warm pitas, for serving

Prepare the mushrooms: In a large bowl, whisk together 4 tablespoons of the olive oil, the garlic, tomato paste, mustard, sugar, cumin, paprika, cinnamon, and a big pinch of salt (see Note). Add the mushrooms and shallots to the marinade and toss to coat. Marinate for 15 minutes.

Preheat the oven to 425°F. Line two baking sheets with parchment paper.

Divide the marinated mushroom mixture between the baking sheets, spreading them out in an even layer and leaving a bit of space between the mushrooms.

Roast until the mushrooms have darkened and reduced in size, 25 to 30 minutes. Drizzle the remaining 2 tablespoons olive oil over the mushrooms. Use a pair of tongs to toss and coat the mushrooms in the oil, roast again until the shallots are caramelized and the mushrooms look deeply browned and a bit crispy, 8 to 10 minutes.

Make the Shirazi salad: In a medium bowl, toss together the tomatoes, cucumbers, shallot, parsley, olive oil, vinegar, and a hefty pinch of salt. Taste and adjust the seasoning as needed.

Make the garlicky yogurt: In a small bowl, stir together the yogurt, dill, garlic, vinegar, and salt. Taste and adjust the seasoning as needed.

To serve: Pile the mushrooms into the warm pitas and top with the salad and garlic sauce. Serve right away.

Note: *Don't be intimidated by the lengthy ingredient list for the mushroom marinade; if you're missing an ingredient or two, replace them with stuff you already have on hand. Out of cinnamon? Use a tiny bit of ground clove. No ketchup? Try using your favorite hot sauce or a dollop of tomato paste.*

Hungarian Lecsó
(Paprika-Packed Pepper Stew)

Serves 4 | Prep Time: 15 minutes | Cook Time: 1 hour | Total Time: 1 hour 15 minutes

Can a simple stew of onions, peppers, and tomatoes really be all that good? I'm here to tell you, oh yes it can! Lecsó (pronounced lech-o) is a staple in any Hungarian household—a modest but oh-so-flavorful pepper stew I grew up with. The sweet smell of simmering peppers, onions, and tomatoes never fails to bring me back to my childhood.

This classic Hungarian dish encompasses so much about the cuisine I was raised with, proving how a handful of humble ingredients can come together and create a magical dish. With a little time and patience, the vegetables and spices cook down into a silky, jammy stew. There are as many versions of this dish as you might imagine: Some families pair it with meat, some with rice, but my family kept things simple and served it with crusty bread, or sometimes a crispy fried egg on top if we were feeling frisky.

¼ cup neutral oil, such as sunflower or grapeseed

3 medium yellow onions (about 1½ pounds), thinly sliced

Kosher salt

4 garlic cloves, chopped

1 tablespoon sweet paprika

½ teaspoon cayenne pepper, plus more to taste

4 medium sweet red bell or yellow Hungarian peppers (about 1½ pounds), sliced

1 (28-ounce) can whole peeled tomatoes

Crusty bread, such as sourdough bread, country loaf, or ciabatta, for serving

Fresh parsley, for serving

In a large pot, heat the oil over medium heat until quite hot, nearly smoking. Add the onions and a big pinch of salt and cook, stirring, until the onions are translucent and soft, 4 to 5 minutes. If the oil sputters too much or the onions begin to burn, reduce the heat to medium-low as needed. Add the garlic, paprika, and cayenne and cook until fragrant, 1 to 2 minutes. Return the heat to medium if you reduced it earlier and add the peppers and another pinch of salt. Cook, stirring occasionally, until quite soft, about 15 minutes.

Add the canned tomatoes, crushing them with your hands as you add them, or breaking them up with a wooden spoon. Bring the mixture to a boil. Reduce the heat to medium-low and simmer until most of the liquid has evaporated and the mixture has a stewy, jammy consistency, 25 to 30 minutes. You can add additional splashes of water to reach the desired consistency. Taste and add salt as needed.

Serve hot, with plenty of crusty bread and parsley.

Note: *If you're looking to revamp any lecsó leftovers, this pepper stew makes a flavor-packed base for a soup. In a medium pot, cook a shallot and a few cloves of garlic until softened, then add a dollop of pepper stew alongside some rotisserie chicken meat, uncooked small pasta such as ditalini or Israeli couscous, torn kale leaves, and chicken stock. Season with salt, pepper, maybe more paprika, and simmer until the pasta is fully cooked. And look! Dinner is sorted.*

One-Pot Baked Risotto
with Blistered Tomatoes and Burrata

Serves 4 to 6 | Prep Time: 10 minutes | Cook Time: 50 minutes | Total Time: 1 hour

Risotto is a slow-cooked, creamy, dreamy Italian rice porridge, flavored with ingredients like wine, some type of stock, lots of butter, and finely grated cheese. If that doesn't describe the most comforting meal, I don't know what does.

However, risotto usually involves you next to the stove babysitting the rice, adding ladle after ladle of stock, mixing constantly for about 40 minutes until the rice has absorbed all the liquid. Instead, here we mix the rice and flavorful blistered tomatoes with all the stock and bake in the oven until the rice absorbs most of the liquid. No stirring, totally hands-off. Top it all off with fresh burrata and let that cream ooze all over.

¼ teaspoon fennel seeds

4 tablespoons extra-virgin olive oil, plus more for serving

1 small bunch fresh oregano or thyme (5 to 8 sprigs)

2 pints or 1½ pounds cherry tomatoes

Kosher salt

1 medium shallot, finely chopped

1 heaping tablespoon tomato paste

1 cup Arborio rice

1 teaspoon freshly ground black pepper, plus more for serving

1 teaspoon red chile flakes

¼ cup red wine or water

1 garlic head, top cut off to expose the cloves, root attached

1 cup (3 ounces) finely grated Parmesan cheese

3 tablespoons unsalted butter

8 ounces burrata cheese, drained

Flaky salt, for serving

Preheat the oven to 375°F.

In a mortar and pestle, crush the fennel seeds roughly. (You can also do this by putting the seeds in a zip-seal plastic bag or between layers of a kitchen towel and going over them a few times with a rolling pin.)

In a large heavy-bottomed Dutch oven, combine 1 tablespoon of the oil and the oregano and cook over medium heat, stirring frequently, for 2 minutes. Add the tomatoes and a hefty pinch of kosher salt and toss to coat the tomatoes in the oil. Partially cover the pot with a lid to keep the oil from splattering. Let the tomatoes cook, undisturbed, until blistered and slightly browned on one side, 4 to 6 minutes. Stir the tomatoes, replace the lid, and cook until the tomatoes are blistered all over and quite browned, 3 to 5 minutes. Scoop out about 1 cup of the tomatoes and reserve for plating.

Add the shallot and tomato paste to the Dutch oven and toss with the blistered tomatoes. Cook until the tomato paste is darkened, about 2 minutes. If the browned bits at the bottom of the pan start cooking too fast, add a splash of water and scrape up those bits with a wooden spoon. Add the remaining 3 tablespoons oil, plus the rice, black pepper, chile flakes, and crushed fennel seeds and cook until the rice is coated in the oil and the spices are fragrant, about 2 minutes. Add the wine and stir for 1 minute. Add 4 cups water and a big pinch of kosher salt and bring to a boil. Halve the garlic head and place the halves on top of the rice mixture, cover the pot with a lid, and transfer to the oven.

Bake until the rice has absorbed all the liquid, 30 to 35 minutes.

Discard the herb sprigs, squeeze in the garlic cloves and discard the skins. Add the Parmesan and butter and stir until the cheese and butter are fully incorporated. If needed, add a splash of water to loosen the risotto. Taste and season with more kosher salt as needed.

Tear the burrata right onto the risotto and top with the reserved blistered tomatoes, lots of olive oil, flaky salt, and black pepper.

Divide the risotto among bowls and serve right away.

Chickpea Artichoke Croquettes

Makes 18 to 22 croquettes | Prep Time: 30 minutes, plus 1 hour chilling | Cook Time: 30 minutes | Total Time: 2 hours

One of my favorite dinners is, well, appetizers. This particular recipe is a vegetarian version of the famous Spanish croquetas. They're crunchy on the outside and soft and cheesy on the inside, thanks to a thick béchamel sauce studded with artichokes, salty briny olives, crushed chickpeas, and melty Manchego. Shaping them feels a bit like playing with slime, so if you're in the right mood for it, making this will be relaxing.

You will need time and energy to make these. They don't make a quick dinner and require some planning ahead. It was one of the few exceptions in the book where I was like, "Yes, the lengthy process will be worth the time," and it will be!

Croquette Mixture

1 teaspoon coriander seeds

½ teaspoon black peppercorns

⅓ cup extra-virgin olive oil

2 small shallots, thinly sliced

3 small fresh red or green chiles, thinly sliced

6 garlic cloves, finely chopped

¾ cup all-purpose flour, plus more as needed

1½ cups whole milk

Kosher salt

5 ounces Manchego cheese, rind removed, cut into ¼-inch cubes

1 (16-ounce) jar kalamata, Castelvetrano, or other olives, drained, pitted, and halved

1 (14-ounce) can quartered artichoke hearts, drained and patted dry

2 (15-ounce) cans chickpeas, drained, rinsed, and patted dry

Make the croquette mixture: In a mortar and pestle, crush the coriander seeds and peppercorns roughly. (You can also do this by putting the spices in between layers of paper towel and going over them a few times with a rolling pin.)

In a medium saucepan, combine the oil, shallots, and chiles and cook over medium heat, stirring occasionally, until soft and translucent, 4 to 5 minutes. Add the garlic and the coriander/black pepper mix, and cook, stirring frequently, until fragrant, 1 to 2 minutes. Add the flour and cook, vigorously stirring, until it darkens and smells a bit toasty, about 2 minutes. Add the milk a splash at a time, stirring constantly until all the milk has been incorporated. Add a big pinch of kosher salt and continue cooking, stirring frequently, until the mixture forms into a big, smooth ball and has a thick paste-like texture, about 3 minutes.

Transfer the mixture to a large bowl, spreading it all over the sides. Set aside for 10 minutes to cool.

Add the Manchego, olives, artichokes, and chickpeas, roughly crushing half of the chickpeas using your hands as you add them (there's truly no better way to do this). Vigorously stir using a spatula or squeeze with your hands to incorporate everything into the paste. It should feel like thick mashed potatoes with other bits in it.

Lightly wet your hands, grab a small handful of the mixture, and shape it into a ball—if it feels gluey and holds together well, you're good. If it's too loose, mix in 1 tablespoon of flour. Repeat, checking the thickness and adding a little flour at a time, up to an extra ¼ cup of flour. Refrigerate for at least 50 minutes, or until firm.

Make the yogurt dill dipping sauce: In a medium bowl, whisk together the yogurt, jalapeño, dill, a pinch of kosher salt, and a splash of water to loosen the sauce. Taste and adjust the salt. Refrigerate until ready to serve.

Yogurt Dill Dipping Sauce

¾ cup whole-milk yogurt

1 large jalapeño or serrano chile, finely chopped

1 tablespoon finely chopped fresh dill

Kosher salt

Breading

3 large eggs

Kosher salt and freshly ground black pepper

1 cup all-purpose flour

1½ cups panko or other bread crumbs

3 tablespoons sesame seeds (optional)

Neutral oil, such as sunflower or grapeseed, for shallow-frying

Flaky salt

Lemon wedges, for serving

Make the breading: Set up a breading station with a shallow bowl and two plates. In the bowl, whisk the eggs with a pinch of kosher salt and a few grinds of pepper. On one shallow plate, combine the flour and a big pinch of salt. On the second plate, toss together the panko and sesame seeds (if using).

Set a clean baking sheet near you to hold the croquettes as you shape them. Fill a small bowl with water and lightly wet your hands. Grab enough croquette mixture to form a two-bite–size croquette. Shape the croquette into a small oblong potato-like shape, 3 to 3½ inches in length. If it looks a little weird, remember fried things are very forgiving when covered up in a crispy coating. Drop the croquette into the flour mixture and toss and roll it around to coat. Set aside on the clean baking sheet. Repeat with the remaining mixture, wetting your hands, shaping the croquettes, coating in the flour, and setting on the baking sheet.

Next, toss a floured croquette in the egg, then add it to the panko mixture to coat, gently patting in the bread crumbs to help them stick. Return the breaded croquette to the baking sheet and repeat with the remaining floured croquettes. Feel free to freeze some for later in a zip-seal bag. You can fry them directly from the freezer next time you're in the mood for some veg croquettes.

Set a wire rack over a baking sheet and place it near the stove. Pour 1 inch of oil into a deep medium pot and heat over medium-high heat until nearly smoking hot, or until a thermometer measures 375°F.

Working in batches of about 4 croquettes, carefully add them to the hot oil and fry until golden brown, 3 to 5 minutes. Flip and fry until crispy and golden all over, 2 to 4 minutes. Using tongs or a slotted spoon, transfer the croquettes to the wire rack. Season with flaky salt right away. Repeat with the remaining croquettes, adjusting the heat as needed to maintain a constant oil temperature.

Serve the croquettes hot with the cool, creamy dipping sauce and lemon wedges on the side.

Butter Beans alla Vodka

Serves 4 | Prep Time: 15 minutes | Cook Time: 25 minutes | Total Time: 40 minutes

Who doesn't love an easy meal you can whip up after a long day with ingredients you already have in your kitchen? This saucy, comforting bean dish stew is just that. In a world where beans become brownies, pastas, and burgers, serving them whole with a pasta sauce feels rebellious. And don't skip the garlic-rubbed toast! It really ties everything together.

Whether you're sharing this or not, I love making a whole batch. The simmered leftovers topped with a fried egg are really something to look forward to the next day.

¼ cup extra-virgin olive oil

2 medium shallots, finely chopped

2 heaping tablespoons tomato paste

6 garlic cloves, thinly sliced

1 teaspoon red chile flakes

2 tablespoons vodka or water

2 (15-ounce) cans butter beans or lima beans, drained and rinsed (see Note)

1 cup heavy cream or full-fat coconut milk

½ cup finely grated Parmesan cheese

4 tablespoons unsalted butter (optional)

Kosher salt and freshly ground black pepper

For Serving

Sliced crusty bread, such as ciabatta, sourdough bread, or any country loaf

1 garlic clove, halved

Extra-virgin olive oil, for drizzling

Grated Parmesan cheese

Red chile flakes

Chopped fresh parsley leaves (optional)

In a medium saucepan, heat the olive oil over medium heat. Add the shallots and cook until translucent and softened, 3 to 4 minutes. Add the tomato paste and cook, stirring occasionally, until fragrant and darkened to a burgundy color, another 3 to 4 minutes. Reduce the heat to medium-low and add the garlic and chile flakes. Cook, stirring constantly, until the garlic is softened and fragrant, just a minute or so. Add the vodka and stir, letting the liquid help you scrape up any bits from the bottom of the pan.

Add the beans, cream, and ½ cup water. Increase the heat to medium-high and bring to a boil. Reduce the heat to a healthy simmer, about medium-low, and cook, stirring occasionally, until the sauce has reduced and looks smooth and glossy, 15 to 20 minutes. Add a splash or two of water to thin the sauce if desired.

Stir in the Parmesan, butter (if using), and a hefty pinch of salt and pepper. Remove the pot from the heat.

To serve: Toast the bread as desired and rub all over with the cut side of the garlic clove. Serve the beans hot with a drizzle of olive oil. Top with more grated Parmesan, chile flakes, and parsley (if using). Serve the garlicky toast on the side.

Note: *If you can't get your hands on butter (or lima) beans, garbanzo or Great Northern beans will work just as well.*

Cheesy Scalloped Tomatoes

Serves 6 to 8 | Prep Time: 15 minutes | Cook Time: 1 hour | Total Time: 1 hour 15 minutes

This is one of those old forgotten recipes I come back to whenever I find myself with a bunch of dried old bread on hand. It's a passed-down family recipe, reminiscent of a savory bread pudding—crusty bread is smothered with tomatoes and cheese and then baked. The bread absorbs all the tart tomato juices, rehydrating in the oven, getting soggy and custardy in the best way possible. Not only is this a great way to give stale bread a second chance, but it's a comforting dish that comes together strictly out of pantry staples and you can come back to it again and again. You might find yourself deliberately leaving your bread out to dry so you can make this for dinner—it's that good!

Neutral oil, for the pan

3 cups (6 ounces) stale crusty bread pieces, cut or torn into big cubes (see Notes)

2 (28-ounce) cans whole peeled tomatoes

1 medium shallot, finely chopped

4 garlic cloves, finely grated

½ teaspoon red chile flakes (optional)

Kosher salt

6 ounces low-moisture mozzarella cheese, coarsely grated

6 ounces extra-sharp cheddar cheese, coarsely grated

Preheat the oven to 325°F. Grease the bottom of a 9-inch square or 8 × 10-inch baking pan with oil.

Add about half of the bread cubes to the baking pan. Using your hands, roughly crush half of the whole peeled tomatoes (1 can's worth) into smaller chunks over the bread cubes. Evenly sprinkle with half of the shallot, half of the garlic, and all the chile flakes (if using). Pour the tomato juices remaining in the can all over the stale bread and season with a hefty pinch of salt all over. It will feel like a lot of liquid, but the stale bread will soak it all up in the oven. Evenly distribute half of the mozzarella and half of the cheddar on top.

Repeat the layering process with the remaining ingredients, except for the cheese in this order: bread, crushed tomatoes from the remaining can, shallot, garlic, canned tomato juices, and a hefty pinch of salt. Reserve the remaining cheese for later.

Bake the scalloped tomatoes until the bread is slightly crunchy on top, about 50 minutes.

Remove the pan from the oven and sprinkle the reserved cheese all over the dish. Return to the oven and bake until the cheese on top is fully melted, 8 to 10 minutes.

Serve hot.

Notes:

- *If your bread is too stale to be torn apart by hand, place the bread in a zip-seal bag and crush it into chunks using a rolling pin.*

- *If you don't have any stale bread on hand but want to make this dish as soon as possible, you can buy some fresh crusty bread from the store, tear it into big chunks, and toast it dry in the oven at 400°F for 8 to 12 minutes, or until the bread has lost most of its moisture content.*

Broccoli Cheddar Beans
with Crispy Cheddar Panko

Serves 4 to 6 | Prep Time: 30 minutes | Cook Time: 30 minutes | Total Time: 1 hour

This recipe takes a classic broccoli cheddar soup and transforms it into a heartier, stewy bean number. I wanted to incorporate that comforting feel of a broccoli cheddar soup into something with more body and texture. Canned butter beans were the perfect addition; they're my go-to bean in soups or stews. I love the way they hold their shape, even when simmered in a sauce.

    The cherry on top is my cheddar panko crumbs: The crunchy clusters add the perfect texture to each bite and highlight the extra sharp cheddar flavor in the stew.

Cheddar Panko

2½ ounces sharp cheddar cheese, coarsely grated (about 1 cup)

½ cup panko or other bread crumbs

2 tablespoons unsalted butter, melted

Broccoli Cheddar Beans

3 tablespoons unsalted butter

2 medium shallots, finely chopped

Kosher salt

4 garlic cloves, finely chopped

1 small head broccoli, chopped into big chunks, including the stalk (4 to 5 cups)

2 tablespoons all-purpose flour or cornstarch

2¼ cups whole milk, plus more as needed

5 ounces sharp cheddar cheese, coarsely grated (about 2 heaping cups)

3 (15-ounce) cans butter beans or lima beans, drained and rinsed (see Note)

For Serving

Flaky salt

Extra-virgin olive oil (optional)

Freshly ground black pepper (optional)

Aleppo pepper or red chile flakes (optional)

Make the cheddar panko: Preheat the oven to 350°F. Line a baking sheet with parchment paper.

Add the cheddar, panko, and melted butter to the baking sheet and toss lightly with your hands to combine. Shake the pan to even out the bread crumb layer. Bake until the mixture becomes crisp and turns a rich golden color, 8 to 10 minutes. Set aside to cool slightly.

Make the cheddar broccoli beans: In a large saucepan, melt the butter over medium heat. Add the shallots and a big pinch of kosher salt and cook until translucent and soft, about 4 minutes. Add the garlic and cook until fragrant, another minute. Add the broccoli and cook, stirring occasionally, until the broccoli is bright green but still firm, 5 to 6 minutes. Feel free to reduce the heat as needed, and if things start to brown too quickly at the bottom of the pan, add a splash of water to deglaze it.

Add the flour and toss to evenly coat the veggies. Slowly add the milk, stirring constantly, and bring the mixture to a simmer. Cook, stirring frequently, until the broccoli is just tender, about 2 minutes.

Remove the pan from the heat. Add the cheddar to the pan. Using an immersion blender, blend until smooth, though a few chunks are okay. (Alternatively, carefully transfer the broccoli mixture to a blender and add the cheddar. Remove the center plug in the lid of the blender to let steam escape, and blend until smooth. Return the mixture to the pan. If you need extra liquid to help blend everything, add a splash of milk.)

Return the pan to medium heat and bring back to a simmer. Add the beans and a hefty pinch of salt and cook, stirring occasionally, until the beans are warmed through and tender, 5 to 8 minutes. Taste and adjust the seasoning.

Divide the bean stew among bowls and crumble the cheddar panko on top and top with flaky salt. If desired, garnish with a drizzle of olive oil, some black pepper, and Aleppo pepper.

Note: *If you can't get your hands on butter (or lima) beans, garbanzo or Great Northern beans will work just as well.*

Paprikash-Inspired Chickpea Stew
with Dumplings

Serves 4 to 6 | Prep Time: 25 minutes | Cook Time: 55 minutes | Total Time: 1 hour 20 minutes

I grew up eating paprikash, a Hungarian stew typically made with chicken drumsticks or thighs simmered in a creamy, bright red paprika sauce. In this vegetarian version, I use chickpeas instead of the traditional chicken. Chickpeas are great at taking on whichever flavor you toss them in; here, they get more savory and peppery the longer they simmer in the broth. Crush some of them to thicken the liquid and watch these beans bring a wonderful texture and body to the stew.

The egg dumplings are very easy, fun to make, and definitely worth the extra 10 minutes it takes to whip them up. They're chewy but tender, and all the nooks and crannies get filled with the paprikash sauce.

Lastly, I grew up eating paprikash with a bunch of scallions—they're crunchy, refreshing, and perfect to cut through the richness of the stew.

Crispy Chickpea Topping

2 (15-ounce) cans chickpeas, drained and rinsed

2 tablespoons extra-virgin olive oil or sunflower oil

2 teaspoons sweet paprika

Kosher salt

Creamy Chickpea Paprikash

¼ cup extra-virgin olive oil or sunflower oil

1 medium yellow onion, finely chopped

2 large red bell peppers, finely chopped

Kosher salt

5 garlic cloves, finely chopped or grated

3 tablespoons sweet paprika

1 heaping tablespoon tomato paste

½ teaspoon cayenne pepper, plus more to taste

2 (15-ounce) cans chickpeas, drained and rinsed

1¾ cups heavy cream or 1 (14-ounce) can full-fat coconut milk

1 tablespoon cornstarch

Make the crispy chickpea topping: Preheat the oven to 425°F. Line a baking sheet with parchment paper.

Add the chickpeas to the baking sheet and roll a kitchen or paper towel over them to remove excess moisture. Drizzle the olive oil on top and add the paprika and a pinch of salt. Toss to coat.

Roast until the chickpeas are crunchy and golden, about 20 minutes.

Meanwhile, make the creamy chickpea paprikash: In a large Dutch oven or saucepan, heat the olive oil over medium heat. Add the onion and cook, stirring frequently, until softened and golden, 8 to 12 minutes. Add the bell peppers and a pinch of salt and cook, stirring occasionally, until softened, about 10 minutes. Add the garlic, paprika, tomato paste, and cayenne and cook, stirring constantly, until the tomato paste has darkened and the spices and garlic are fragrant, about 2 minutes.

Add the chickpeas and toss to coat in the spices, adding a splash of water and stirring to break up the browned bits at the bottom of the pan. Cook to let the chickpeas warm through and absorb some of the flavors, about 3 minutes. Stir in the cream, a hefty pinch of salt, and 1½ cups water and bring to a simmer. Reduce the heat to medium-low and simmer, stirring occasionally, until the chickpeas are soft and flavorful, 25 to 30 minutes.

In a small bowl, whisk the cornstarch with 2 tablespoons water. Add the cornstarch slurry to the soup and continue simmering, stirring constantly, until thickened, 4 to 5 minutes. Crush some of the chickpeas against the side of the pot with the back of the spoon. Remove the pan from the heat and cover to keep warm.

(recipe continues)

Egg Dumplings

Kosher salt

6 large eggs

2 cups all-purpose flour

Sliced scallions, for serving

Make the egg dumplings: Bring a large saucepan of well-salted water to a boil over medium-high heat.

In a medium bowl, whisk together the eggs, flour, and a pinch of salt until smooth. The mixture should have the consistency of a thick, gloopy pancake batter. Feel free to add a splash of water or a bit more flour to adjust the consistency.

Using a spoon, scrape a little bit of the batter—just 1 or 2 teaspoons (the batter expands as it cooks)—against the side of the bowl, directly into the boiling water. Dip the spoon in the boiling water and repeat the scraping motion with the remaining batter. Boil the dumplings until they float, about 3 minutes. Remove the pan from the heat, cover, and let sit for 5 minutes. Drain the dumplings.

Divide the dumplings among bowls and ladle the creamy chickpea stew alongside them. Top with the crispy chickpeas and lots of crunchy fresh scallions.

Note: *You really shouldn't skip the egg dumplings, as they're the ideal accompaniment to the stew, though some plain white rice or egg noodles would make a great substitute.*

Mushroom Kale Veggie Burgers
with Horseradish Mayo

Serves 6 | Prep Time: 20 minutes, plus 4 hours chilling | Cook Time: 1 hour 40 minutes | Total Time: 6 hours

I've got some serious beef with veggie burgers—no pun intended. They always sound so good and enticing, packed with fresh, delicious veggies, until you take a bite just to be hit with stodgy, dull mush. I understand the need for processing them in a blender or food processor to have them stick together somehow, but there has to be a way to keep whole bites of veggies together in a patty-like shape, right? Instead of mashing them all up, what if you had a cluster of vegetables instead?

That's the recipe I developed for all of you texture-seekers. While it will be more time-consuming than throwing things in a blender and frying a patty, this recipe promises texture in every bite. Stick it in a grilled cheese sandwich for the ultimate veggie melt, toss onto a burger bun with your favorite sauces and toppings, or simply fry in the morning with a side of eggs.

Veggie Burgers

4 tablespoons extra-virgin olive oil, plus more as needed

1½ pounds mushrooms, torn into chunky bite-size pieces

½ bunch kale, stems finely sliced and leaves separated and chopped

Kosher salt

1 medium yellow onion, roughly chopped

1 (15-ounce) can chickpeas, drained and rinsed

2 tablespoons soy sauce

2 tablespoons balsamic vinegar

2 teaspoons sweet paprika

½ tablespoon Dijon mustard

1 teaspoon red chile flakes

½ cup cornstarch

Horseradish Mayo

⅓ cup mayonnaise

2 teaspoons grated horseradish, fresh or prepared

Kosher salt

For Serving

6 hamburger buns, split

Burger toppings, such as cheese, pickles, sliced tomatoes, crisp lettuce, etc.

Make the veggie burgers: Preheat the oven to 375°F. Lightly grease a 9-inch square baking pan with oil. Then line it with parchment paper, letting the sides hang over an inch or so (to help lift out the mixture later). Lightly brush the parchment paper with oil. Place the pan on a clean baking sheet.

In a large skillet, heat 2 tablespoons of the oil over medium-high heat. Add the mushrooms, kale stems, and a hefty pinch of salt. Cook, stirring frequently, until the mushrooms are a rich brown color and have reduced in size, about 10 minutes. Transfer the mixture to a large bowl.

Return the skillet to medium-high heat and heat 1 more tablespoon of the oil. Add the onion and cook until they have browned slightly but aren't yet translucent, 2 to 3 minutes. Transfer the onions to the bowl with the mushrooms.

Return the skillet to medium heat and heat the remaining 1 tablespoon oil. Add the chickpeas and kale leaves and cook, stirring frequently, until the kale has wilted slightly, 4 to 6 minutes.

Use the back of a wooden spoon to crush about one-third of the chickpeas against the sides of the skillet. Add the soy sauce, vinegar, paprika, mustard, and chile flakes and cook until fragrant, 2 to 3 minutes. Remove the skillet from the heat.

Add the chickpea mixture to the bowl with the onions and mushrooms. Add the cornstarch and another pinch of salt and mix with your hands or a silicone spatula. The mixture should feel dense but gloopy, like a thick batter, so add a few tablespoons of water to help it come together if needed.

(recipe continues)

Add the veggie mixture to the lined baking pan. Use your hands to tightly press it down to evenly distribute in the pan. Place a second sheet of parchment on top and press it down to ensure contact. Weight the mixture down with a second pan or ovenproof plate, whatever will fit right on top of the mixture. (I like using an 8-inch square pan filled halfway with water or packed with grill weights.)

Bake until firm and fragrant, 50 to 55 minutes.

Carefully remove the weighted pan and the top layer of parchment. Increase the oven temperature to 400°F and return the pan to the oven. Roast until the veggie mixture forms a thick dark crust on top, about 15 minutes. Cool completely.

Place a new clean sheet of parchment paper on the mixture and add a weight back on top (whatever you used in the oven is fine). Refrigerate for 4 hours, preferably overnight.

Remove the weight and the top sheet of parchment. Use the sides of the bottom sheet of parchment to pull the chilled veggie mixture out of the pan and cut the mixture into 6 square-ish patties.

In a medium skillet over medium heat, heat a small amount of oil. Cook the patties in batches until they develop a nicely browned crust, 1 to 2 minutes per side. Set aside on a plate and remove the pan from the heat.

Make the horseradish mayo: In a small bowl, combine the mayonnaise, horseradish, and a pinch of salt.

To serve: Slather the burger buns with the horseradish mayo and place a patty on top. Pile on your favorite burger toppings and serve.

soup's on

Coconut Butternut Squash Soup
with Cumin

Serves 4 | Prep Time: 15 minutes | Cook Time: 1 hour | Total Time: 1 hour 15 minutes

This is not another blended butternut squash soup! When I was growing up, my mother made a chilled zucchini soup all summer long—refreshing, creamy, and packed with grated zucchini and fragrant spices like cumin, sweet paprika, and cayenne. My squash soup is the cozier autumnal cousin to the summer squash soup of my memories. I roughly smash some of the coconut-simmered squash, while also preserving some big chunks for texture. I swapped out the heavy cream in my mother's soup for full-fat coconut milk to highlight the inviting sweetness of the squash.

3 tablespoons extra-virgin olive oil

2 medium shallots, finely chopped

3 garlic cloves, chopped

2½ teaspoons cumin seeds

1½ teaspoons sweet paprika

¼ teaspoon cayenne pepper

2 celery stalks, finely chopped

Kosher salt

¼ cup white wine or water

1 small butternut squash (about 1 pound), peeled, seeded, and cut into ½-inch cubes

1 small bunch of fresh parsley

1 (13.5-ounce) can full-fat coconut milk

¼ cup chopped fresh parsley

1½ tablespoons fresh lemon juice

For Serving

Cayenne pepper

Extra-virgin olive oil, for drizzling

Chopped fresh parsley

Warm crusty bread

In a large soup pot, heat the olive oil over medium heat for 2 minutes. Add the shallots and cook, stirring occasionally, until softened and translucent, about 4 minutes. Reduce the heat to medium-low and continue cooking, stirring occasionally, until the shallots are caramelized, with a few crispy edges, 5 to 6 minutes. Add a splash of water to deglaze the pot if needed.

Add the garlic, cumin seeds, paprika, and cayenne and cook, stirring, until fragrant, about 2 minutes. Increase the heat to medium, add the celery and a pinch of salt and cook until softened, about 5 minutes. Add the white wine and stir, scraping up any browned bits from the bottom of the pot. Add the squash and cook, tossing and stirring, until partially softened, 6 to 8 minutes.

Add the bunch of parsley, a big pinch of salt, and 2½ cups water and bring to a boil. Reduce the heat to medium-low and simmer until the squash is fork-tender, 20 to 25 minutes.

Remove and discard the parsley bunch. Using a potato masher, crush about half of the squash in the pot. You're not looking for a totally smooth consistency, just adding some heft. Leave the remaining squash pieces intact. Stir in the coconut milk and simmer until the flavors come together, 5 to 7 minutes. Add more water to thin the soup if needed, and taste and adjust the salt. Remove the pot from the heat. Stir in the chopped parsley and lemon juice.

To serve: Divide the soup among bowls and top with a sprinkle of cayenne, a drizzle of olive oil, and fresh parsley. Serve with crusty bread on the side.

Miso Mushroom Chicken Soup

Serves 4 | Prep Time: 15 minutes | Cook Time: 40 minutes | Total Time: 55 minutes

We all know the excitement of buying a rotisserie chicken: You get home, eat the crispy skin, and snack on half a breast. The next day you revisit it, toss it in a salad or sandwich, but the third day is when the excitement starts to fade. The stress of "how can I keep this from going to waste even though I'm so over it" starts to seep in. What are your options? Another chicken salad? Meh! This soup revives your old rotisserie chicken by transporting it to a mushroomy, salty, creamy miso environment.

¼ cup neutral oil, such as sunflower or grapeseed, plus more as needed

½ pound mixed mushrooms, roughly chopped

Kosher salt and freshly ground black pepper

1 medium shallot, finely chopped

3 garlic cloves, minced or finely grated

½ teaspoon ground turmeric

½ teaspoon cumin seeds

¼ teaspoon cayenne pepper

2 tablespoons soy sauce

1 tablespoon rice vinegar or apple cider vinegar

2½ to 3 cups chopped cooked chicken

1 cup ditalini or any small pasta

2 cups chopped lacinato or green curly kale

1 cup thinly sliced sugar snap peas

2 tablespoons white miso, plus more to taste

In a large soup pot, heat the oil over medium heat. Add the mushrooms, a small pinch of salt, and several grinds of black pepper and cook, stirring frequently, until the mushrooms have cooked down to a rich brown color and released all of their liquid, 10 to 12 minutes. Reduce the heat to medium-low, add the shallot, and cook until softened and translucent, 3 to 4 minutes, adding another tablespoon of oil if the mixture looks dry.

Add the garlic, turmeric, cumin, and cayenne and cook, stirring, until fragrant, 1 to 2 minutes. Stir in the soy sauce and vinegar, scraping any caramelized bits off the bottom of the pot. Add the chicken and cook, stirring and tossing to help it absorb some of the flavors, 3 to 4 minutes. Add 4 cups water, increase the heat to high, and bring to a boil. Reduce the heat to medium-low and simmer, stirring occasionally, for 15 minutes.

Meanwhile, bring a small saucepan of well-salted water to a boil over medium-high heat. Add the pasta and cook for 3 minutes less than what the package calls for. Drain the pasta and set aside.

To the simmering soup, add the kale and snap peas and cook until softened and bright green, about 2 minutes. Remove the pot from the heat and add the cooked pasta.

In a small bowl, combine the miso with a small ladleful of the hot soup. Stir until the mixture is pourable and creamy. Add the miso mixture to the soup and stir to combine. Taste and add more miso as needed (my sweet spot is between 3 and 4 tablespoons).

Divide the soup among bowls, top with lots of freshly ground black pepper, and serve.

Cheesy Potato Soup
with Rosemary Croutons

Serves 4 to 6 | Prep Time: 25 minutes | Cook Time: 25 minutes | Total Time: 50 minutes

Some meals are meant to nourish your body: They're well-balanced, packed with protein and healthy fats, good carbs, yada yada. Some meals are just here to keep you sane and nourish your soul. This cozy, carby soup belongs to the second category. I leaned into the classic potato-rosemary combination by pairing the soup with crunchy, fragrant rosemary croutons (which might be the best part of this recipe). The toasty croutons, with their golden nooks and crunchy crannies, are the perfect textural contrast to the creamy soup.

Soup

3 tablespoons unsalted butter

3 small shallots, chopped

6 garlic cloves, smashed

1 tablespoon chopped fresh rosemary (about 2 sprigs)

½ teaspoon freshly cracked black pepper

½ teaspoon cayenne pepper

2 pounds Yukon Gold potatoes (3 to 4 large potatoes), peeled and cut into 1-inch cubes

2 cups whole milk, plus more as needed

1½ cups vegetable broth or water

Kosher salt

Rosemary Croutons

10 ounces crusty bread, such as country loaf or ciabatta, torn into bite-size pieces

¼ cup extra-virgin olive oil

2 tablespoons chopped fresh rosemary (3 to 4 sprigs)

2 garlic cloves, minced or finely grated

Kosher salt

To Finish

2 cups coarsely grated Gruyère cheese or sharp cheddar (about 4 ounces)

Extra-virgin olive oil, for drizzling

Make the soup: In a medium soup pot, melt the butter over medium heat. Add the shallots and cook, stirring occasionally, until translucent and softened, 3 to 4 minutes. Add the garlic, rosemary, black pepper, and cayenne and sizzle them in the butter until just fragrant, 1 to 2 minutes. Add the potatoes, milk, and broth, plus a big pinch of salt. Increase the heat to high and bring to a boil. Reduce the heat to medium-low and simmer, stirring occasionally, until the potatoes are soft and easily pierced with a fork, about 25 minutes.

Meanwhile, make the rosemary croutons: Preheat the oven to 400°F. Line a baking sheet with parchment paper.

Add the torn bread to a large bowl and toss with the olive oil, rosemary, garlic, and a hefty pinch of salt until thoroughly coated. Arrange the seasoned bread pieces in an even layer on the baking sheet. Bake until the croutons are golden with browned, crunchy edges, 12 to 15 minutes.

To finish the soup: Using a slotted spoon, scoop out and reserve about 1½ cups of the potatoes. Carefully add the remaining soup to a blender and blend until smooth. (Remember to remove the small plug in the middle of the lid before blending to let steam escape. Or you can also do this with an immersion blender.) If the soup feels too thick, add more water or milk until it reaches your desired consistency. Do not overblend, as the soup can turn gloopy. Return the blended soup to the pot.

Add the reserved potatoes and the grated cheese to the soup and stir well to help the residual heat melt the cheese. Taste and adjust the seasonings or consistency as needed.

Divide the soup among bowls and top with a drizzle of olive oil and the freshly baked croutons.

Note: *To keep the croutons crunchy for longer if you have any left over, store them in an airtight container with a silica gel pack, at room temperature. I always save those little packs when I open a pack of seaweed or crunchy snack that comes with one.*

Red Lentil Tomato Soup

Serves 4 to 6 | Prep Time: 20 minutes | Cook Time: 1 hour 35 minutes | Total Time: 1 hour 55 minutes

I'm a big lentil eater—they're extremely versatile, super filling, and a great vegetarian protein source, plus they take on any flavor you want them to take. If you're turning these pages, searching for a porridge-y, soupy, stewy meal, you'll find lots of comfort in this recipe. The lentils are slowly cooked in a tomato broth flavored with lots of savory vegetables and warm spices, such as paprika and cumin, then showered in olive oil drizzles.

Lentil Soup

1½ cups red lentils

4 cups boiling water

¼ cup extra-virgin olive oil

1 medium yellow onion, chopped

4 celery stalks, finely chopped

2 medium carrots, finely chopped

Kosher salt

8 garlic cloves, chopped

2 teaspoons dried oregano

2 teaspoons sweet paprika

1 teaspoon ground cumin

½ teaspoon cayenne pepper, plus more to taste

1 (28-ounce) can whole peeled tomatoes

Freshly ground black pepper

½ cup finely chopped fresh parsley

For Serving

Toasted or fried bread rubbed with fresh garlic

Extra-virgin olive oil

Chopped fresh parsley

Grated Parmesan cheese (optional)

In a heatproof medium bowl, cover the lentils with the boiling water and set aside.

In a large soup pot, heat the oil over medium-high heat. Add the onion, celery, carrots, and a pinch of salt and cook, stirring occasionally, until the vegetables have softened and caramelized, 10 to 12 minutes. Add the garlic, oregano, paprika, cumin, and cayenne and cook, stirring frequently, until fragrant, 2 to 3 minutes.

Drain and rinse the lentils under running water. Add the lentils to the pot, along with the tomatoes, a big pinch of salt, and several grinds of black pepper and stir to combine. Use the back of a spoon to crush the tomatoes against the sides of the pot. Using one of the empty tomato cans, measure and add 2 cans of water (about 7 cups total). Bring to a boil and reduce the heat to medium-low. Simmer, stirring occasionally, until the lentils are soft, tender, and broken down and the soup has visibly thickened, 1 to 1½ hours. You can add more water as needed to reach your desired consistency. Season with more salt, black pepper, or cayenne as needed. Remove the pot from the heat and stir in the parsley.

Divide the soup among bowls and serve with toasted or fried bread rubbed with garlic, a drizzle of olive oil, a sprinkle of parsley, and grated Parmesan (if using).

Note: *The leftovers are just as inviting the next day; I like to have a warm bowl of this soup with soft, poached eggs broken right on top for breakfast.*

Hearty White Bean Soup
with Crispy Fennel

Serves 4 to 6 | Prep Time: 25 minutes | Cook Time: 1 hour 20 minutes | Total Time: 1 hour 45 minutes

You're probably tired of reading my thoughts on butter beans being the superior bean. I'll save that mono-logue for my other bean-forward recipes. Can you ever go wrong with a bean soup, though?! I could have this on any occasion. Start with a mountain of finely shaved onions for the base that's cooked until melty and soft. The savory, fennel-spiced broth gets topped with finely shaved sweet fennel roasted with crunchy panko for a boost of texture.

White Bean Soup

1½ teaspoons fennel seeds

1 teaspoon black peppercorns

1 teaspoon coriander seeds

¼ cup extra-virgin olive oil

2 medium yellow onions, finely chopped

Kosher salt

5 celery stalks, finely chopped

6 garlic cloves, thinly sliced

⅓ cup white wine or water

4 (15-ounce) cans butter beans or lima beans, drained and rinsed (see Note)

Crispy Fennel Topping

1 medium fennel bulb, thinly sliced

3 tablespoons extra-virgin olive oil

⅓ cup panko or other bread crumbs

Kosher salt

For Serving

Rice vinegar or apple cider vinegar (optional)

Extra-virgin olive oil, for drizzling

Make the white bean soup: In a mortar and pestle, roughly crush the fen-nel seeds, peppercorns, and coriander seeds. (You can also do this by put-ting the spices in a zip-seal plastic bag or between layers of a kitchen towel and going over them a few times with a rolling pin.)

In a large soup pot, heat the oil over medium-high heat. Add the onions and a big pinch of salt and cook, stirring occasionally, until soft and golden, 5 to 8 minutes. Add the celery and continue cooking, stirring occasionally, until the celery is lighter green and softened, 8 to 10 minutes. Add the gar-lic and the crushed fennel/peppercorn/coriander mix and cook, stirring, until fragrant, about 2 minutes. Add the wine and use a wooden spoon to scrape up any browned bits from the bottom of the pot.

Add the drained beans, a big pinch of salt, and 4½ cups water and bring to a simmer. Reduce the heat to medium-low and simmer, stirring occasion-ally. As the soup cooks, crush some of the beans by pressing them against the sides of the pot with the back of a wooden spoon. Simmer until the soup has thickened and the flavors have combined, 40 to 45 minutes. If the soup thickens too quickly, add a splash of water to reach your desired consistency. Taste and adjust the salt. Remove the pot from the heat.

Meanwhile, make the crispy fennel topping: Preheat the oven to 400°F. Line a baking sheet with parchment paper.

Lay the sliced fennel on the baking sheet and drizzle it with the oil. Scat-ter the panko and some salt on top and use your hands to toss and coat the fennel.

Roast until the fennel is tender and frizzled around the edges and the panko is golden and crisp, 18 to 20 minutes.

To serve: Divide the soup among bowls. If desired, add a splash of vinegar to each bowl. Top with the crispy roasted fennel and a drizzle of olive oil.

Note: *If you can't get your hands on butter (or lima) beans, garbanzo or Great Northern beans will work just as well.*

Roasted Cherry Tomato Soup

Makes 4 to 6 servings | Prep Time: 15 minutes | Cook Time: 40 minutes | Total Time: 55 minutes

Is there anything more comforting than a creamy tomato soup with crunchy toasted bread? My roasted cherry tomato soup recipe has gotten so much love over the years, it had to make it into the cookbook. Initially, I wanted to change things up, use another tomato variety, whip up a bunch of toppings, all the fun stuff. I used canned tomatoes for a smoother mouthfeel, but started missing the teeny charred tomato skins. A few days later, I realized the recipe didn't need upgrades. This tomato soup was so approachable, and loved, from the first day because of its simplicity and effortless feel, so I wanted to preserve that.

3 pounds cherry tomatoes

4 medium shallots, peeled and quartered

2 medium garlic heads, top cut off to expose the cloves, roots attached

4 sprigs fresh rosemary (optional)

2 red Fresno chiles, chopped (optional)

½ cup extra-virgin olive oil

Kosher salt and freshly ground black pepper

1 cup heavy cream or full-fat coconut milk

1 cup vegetable broth or water

Handful of fresh basil leaves, torn (optional)

Toasted crusty bread, for serving

Preheat the oven to 425°F.

On a large baking sheet, combine the tomatoes, shallots, garlic, rosemary (if using), and chiles (if using). Add the olive oil, salt generously, sprinkle black pepper all over, and toss to coat. Arrange everything in an even layer, ensuring the shallots and garlic are cut-side down.

Roast until the tomatoes are slightly blistered and charred and the shallots are soft and translucent, 30 to 40 minutes. Squeeze the roasted garlic out of their skins over the tomatoes, and if you added rosemary, remove and discard it now.

Carefully transfer the tomato mixture to a blender or food processor. Add the cream, broth, and basil (if using). If you're using a blender, remove the plug from the lid to let excess steam escape, and cover with a kitchen towel. Blend until completely smooth. Taste and adjust the salt as needed.

Serve immediately with toasted bread.

Note: *If you find yourself with leftovers on hand, consider next day's breakfast sorted. Heat up a cup of soup in a pan, crack in a couple of eggs, and cover with a lid to steam the eggs. Once the egg whites look opaque, remove the pan from the heat. Poke the jammy yolks with some crusty toasted bread and swirl them around with the soup. That said, this soup keeps very well in the freezer.*

Classic Chicken Noodle Soup

Serves 6 | Prep Time: 10 minutes | Cook Time: 1 hour 15 minutes | Total Time: 1 hour 25 minutes

When I say I was raised on this, I really do mean I ate it for breakfast, lunch, and dinner. In fact, shopping for handmade noodles was one of the first lessons I got on tipping and supporting local craftspeople. Some of my earliest memories involve walking through the farmers' market, my mother explaining to me how the sweet old ladies we bought our noodles from made them by hand. She stressed what a craft it is and how we should always pay them a big tip to encourage and sustain their work. She'd always pass me the tip and make me go up to the ladies and thank them—a precious experience.

Chicken Broth

2 tablespoons neutral oil, such as sunflower or grapeseed

2 medium yellow onions, unpeeled, halved through the root

1 medium head garlic, halved horizontally

1½ to 2 pounds bone-in, skin-on chicken thighs

Any additional chicken scraps, such as bones, neck, feet, etc. (optional)

5 celery stalks, cut into chunks

3 medium carrots, cut into chunks

1 small (2- to 3-ounce) bunch fresh flat-leaf parsley

1 tablespoon black peppercorns

2 teaspoons chicken bouillon powder or 1 chicken bouillon cube

Kosher salt

For Serving

Grated fresh garlic

8 ounces noodles of choice, cooked

Chopped fresh parsley

Freshly ground black pepper

Red chile flakes (optional)

Make the chicken broth: In a large stockpot, heat the oil over medium heat for 2 minutes. Place the onion and garlic halves cut-side down in the pot and sear, undisturbed, until they develop a little bit of color, about 2 minutes. Add the chicken thighs, plus any chicken bones or other parts (if using), and 12 cups water. Increase the heat to medium-high and bring to a boil.

As the broth starts to boil, you'll notice some foam rise to the top. Fill a medium bowl with water and, using a skimmer or small fine-mesh strainer, skim the foam off the stock and dip the skimmer in the bowl of water. Repeat until most of the foam has been removed, changing the water in the bowl as needed to keep the skimmer clean.

Add the celery, carrots, parsley bunch, peppercorns, and bouillon. Reduce the heat to low and simmer, partially covered, for 1 hour.

Using tongs or a skimmer, remove all of the chicken pieces, vegetables, and parsley from the soup and transfer to a bowl. My family always gathered around the chicken soup scrap bowl, snacking on the veggies and the hot, freshly boiled chicken, sprinkled with salt. You can choose to do that, or discard the vegetables and reserve the chicken for serving in the soup.

Add 1 tablespoon salt to the soup, stir well, and taste, adding more salt as needed. Remember, you're seasoning a *lot* of liquid, so you'll need a lot of salt (the sweet spot for me is 2 to 2½ tablespoons Diamond Crystal kosher salt). You should be left with 2 to 2½ quarts (8 to 10 cups) of liquid.

To serve: I like grating a bit of garlic into a bowl—the heat of the soup will cook the garlic and it creates the most inviting aroma! Add the cooked noodles to the bowl and ladle the hot broth over the noodles. Top with parsley, freshly cracked black pepper, and red chile flakes (if using).

Zingy Sour Veggie Soup

Serves 4 to 6 | Prep Time: 15 minutes | Cook Time: 45 minutes | Total Time: 1 hour

While I was growing up, a very important family tradition was making homemade sauerkraut during wintertime. Imagine a week-long process, including buying dozens of cabbages, chopping them, massaging in cups of salt, and fermenting. For the first days, the two fifty-liter barrels would take up our entire kitchen—I still remember that pungent smell. Once the cabbage was sour, we'd transfer the barrels to our tiny balcony to sit all winter. From there, my family would scoop handfuls and handfuls of it for dinner, make soups out of it, stir-fry it with beef or chicken, use it in cabbage rolls, or simply drink the fermented, salty brine.

This is one of the recipes my mother would make all winter long with our homemade sauerkraut: grated veggies and sauerkraut simmered in that sour, zingy brine. We'd have this for breakfast, with bread and black pepper on top. It's hearty, comforting, and so flavorful. Don't worry, I won't call for a hundred liters of sauerkraut; I tailored the recipe to use just one store-bought jar.

Sour Veggie Soup

3 tablespoons neutral oil, such as sunflower or grapeseed

2 medium shallots, finely chopped

3 medium carrots, coarsely grated (about 1 heaping cup)

2 medium zucchini, coarsely grated (about 2 cups)

Kosher salt

2 tablespoons tomato paste

1 teaspoon sweet paprika

1 teaspoon red chile flakes

1 (16-ounce) jar sauerkraut, undrained

1 garlic head, top cut off to expose the cloves, root attached

For Serving

Chopped fresh dill or parsley

Freshly ground black pepper

Crusty bread

Make the sour veggie soup: In a large soup pot, heat the oil over medium heat. Add the shallots and cook until soft and translucent, 3 to 4 minutes. Add the carrots, zucchini, and a pinch of salt and cook, stirring occasionally, until the vegetables are tender, 8 to 10 minutes. Add the tomato paste, paprika, and chile flakes and cook, stirring constantly, until the tomato paste darkens, about 3 minutes.

Add all the sauerkraut from the jar, juices and all, plus 6 cups water and a big pinch of salt and stir to combine. Bring to a boil, reduce the heat to medium-low, and lay the garlic heads, cut-side up, into the soup. Simmer, stirring occasionally, until the soup is slightly thickened and all the vegetables are soft, 25 to 30 minutes. Taste and adjust the seasoning as needed. Remove the pot from the heat and remove and reserve the garlic.

To serve: Divide the soup among bowls and top with fresh herbs and plenty of freshly ground black pepper. I also like to squeeze one or two of the softened garlic cloves in each bowl before serving, but you can leave them out if you like. Serve hot with crusty bread.

salad
days

Sweet and Tart Root Vegetable Salad

Serves 6 to 8 | Prep Time: 35 minutes | Total Time: 35 minutes

At first glance, this salad might not seem special. Root vegetables? Like beets and parsnip? Don't they taste like dirt? With the right dressing, we can brighten them up and bring out their natural sweetness, pairing them with apples, orange juice, and tart vinegar.

My mother would make batches of this salad, storing them in these giant, reused ice cream containers and keeping them in the fridge to serve throughout the week. I still remember the bright pink beet stains on my hands after massaging the dressing into the salad. The longer it chills in the fridge, the better it gets. Unlike a green salad with tender lettuce leaves wilting overnight, this root veg salad will not only last in the fridge for a few days, but will get tastier each day.

1 tablespoon sugar

2 teaspoons grated orange zest (from 1 medium orange)

Kosher salt

3 tablespoons fresh orange juice, plus more to taste

2 tablespoons apple cider vinegar, plus more to taste

2 tablespoons neutral oil, such as sunflower or grapeseed

1 cup coarsely grated carrots (about 2 medium carrots)

1 cup coarsely grated parsnip (about 1 medium parsnip)

1 cup coarsely grated red beet (about 1 medium beet)

1 cup coarsely grated sweet apple (about 2 large apples), such as Honeycrisp or Pink Lady

In a large bowl, combine the sugar, orange zest, and a big pinch of salt. Use your fingers to pinch and rub the mixture together until pale yellow and fragrant. The abrasive texture of the sugar and salt helps extract the flavor and natural oils from the orange zest.

Add the orange juice, vinegar, and oil and whisk to combine. Add the carrots, parsnip, beet, and apples and massage well (see Note), until the vegetables soften, 2 to 3 minutes. Taste and add more vinegar or orange juice to taste.

Serve right away or store in an airtight container in the fridge. This salad gets better the more it sits and soaks up all the juices, so it's a great make-ahead option or something to slowly use up during the week.

Note: *To prevent your hands from staying stained with bright pink beet pigment for days, make sure to wash your hands with warm water and soap as soon as you are done massaging the salad. The longer you let the beet juices stay on your hands, the harder it will be to get them out.*

Creamy Miso Potato Salad

Serves 4 to 6 | Prep Time: 25 minutes, plus 2 hours chilling | Cook Time: 20 minutes |
Total Time: 2 hours 45 minutes

This miso potato salad was the first recipe I saved for the book. It started off as a riff on my mother's infamous winter potato salad. She'd make it with lots of onions, soft boiled chunky potatoes, black olives, and cured salmon. I remember how this cured salmon used to be so expensive and such a treat, so she'd make the salad only once a year.

Instead of her red potatoes, I use baby Yukon Golds, always peeled for a tender mouthfeel. Instead of black olives I went with green Castelvetranos and salty, oily anchovies for the cured salmon. It all comes together with a miso-spiked mayo and is topped with crushed potato chips for the perfect potato-on-potato crunch factor.

Kosher salt

1½ pounds baby Yukon Gold
    potatoes

½ cup mayonnaise

4 to 6 oil-packed anchovy fillets,
    finely chopped (see Note)

3 garlic cloves, minced or finely
    grated

1 small shallot, finely chopped

1 tablespoon white miso, plus
    more to taste

2 tablespoons brined capers,
    rinsed and chopped

2 tablespoons rice vinegar or
    apple cider vinegar

½ cup unpitted Castelvetrano
    olives (see Note)

1 cup kettle-cooked potato chips,
    crushed

¼ cup finely chopped fresh chives

Bring a large saucepan of water to a boil over medium-high heat. Season with a big pinch of salt and add the potatoes. Boil, stirring occasionally, until the potatoes are fork-tender, 20 to 25 minutes. Drain the potatoes and let cool.

In a large bowl, whisk together the mayo, anchovies, garlic, shallot, miso, capers, and vinegar. Taste and add more miso, 1 teaspoon at a time, until the dressing is the perfect balance of creamy, salty, and umami.

Using a paring knife or just your fingers, peel the cooled potatoes—their skins should slip off pretty easily (see Note). Add the peeled potatoes to the large bowl with the dressing.

Crush the olives with the back of a knife, like you'd crush a clove of garlic. Remove the pit, tear the olive in half, and add it to the bowl with the potatoes and dressing.

Toss the potatoes and olives in the dressing to coat. As you mix, crush some of the potatoes with the back of a spoon against the side of the bowl to help bind the salad. Taste and check for seasoning—the dressing might be salty enough, but if not, add a pinch of salt and combine. Cover and refrigerate for at least 2 hours and up to overnight.

Right before serving, top the salad with the crushed potato chips and fresh chives.

Notes:

• *As always, if you're not a fan of anchovies, omit them or add 1 to 2 tablespoons of soy sauce to replicate that salty, umami flavor.*

• *Unpitted olives have a better, more crisp texture, that's why they're my first choice. That said, you can totally start with store-bought pitted olives to save yourself some time.*

• *If you don't feel like peeling all those potatoes, skip it. The creaminess peeled potatoes bring to the salad is incredible, but the salad will absolutely work with unpeeled potatoes.*

Heirloom Tomato Salad
with Anchovy Panko

Serves 4 to 6 | Prep Time: 10 minutes | Cook Time: 10 minutes | Total Time: 20 minutes

Imagine this: It's a summer evening, the sun is almost setting, when a pleasant breeze cuts the heat. You're outside—on a porch, a balcony, someone's backyard—and a platter of juicy, perfectly ripe tomatoes shows up. The garlic smell and freshly torn basil are perfuming the air and you're ready to dive in. But wait! Someone scatters crunchy golden bits all over the platter—garlicky, anchovy panko bits. You take a bite, tomato juices running down your chin, while being met with this crisp texture and umami aroma. You can't help but go back for more, while sipping on crisp white wine.

Anchovy Panko

2 tablespoons extra-virgin olive oil

4 oil-packed anchovy fillets

1 tablespoon anchovy oil (from the tin or jar)

2 garlic cloves, finely chopped

½ cup panko or other bread crumbs

Tomato Salad

1 tablespoon extra-virgin olive oil

1 tablespoon rice vinegar

1 garlic clove, grated

1 pound mixed heirloom and cherry tomatoes

Kosher salt

8 or 10 fresh basil leaves

Make the anchovy panko: In a small pan, combine the olive oil, anchovies, and anchovy oil. Cook over medium heat, stirring occasionally, until most of the anchovies have broken down in the oil, about 2 minutes. If they're still whole, gently break them up with a wooden spoon.

Reduce the heat to medium-low. Add the garlic and cook until fragrant, about 1 minute. Add the panko and toss to coat in the oil. Cook, stirring constantly, until the bread crumbs are fragrant, golden, and crisp, 4 to 6 minutes. Transfer the panko mixture to a plate to cool.

Make the tomato salad: On a large plate, combine the olive oil, vinegar, and garlic and mix briefly. Slice the larger tomatoes into ½-inch slices, halve the cherry tomatoes, and add them to the plate. Season lightly with salt and tear the basil leaves, scattering them on top. Flip the tomatoes gently to coat in the oil and vinegar and rearrange them in an even layer on the plate (there can be some overlap, but you'll want to maximize the available surface area for the delicious bread crumbs!).

Right before serving, top with the garlic anchovy panko mixture, sprinkling it all over the platter. Serve immediately.

Note: *The panko will quickly absorb the tomato juices and lose some of their crunch. If you're feeding a crowd, serve the tomato salad and bread crumbs separately, right next to each other, encouraging your guests to sprinkle on the panko right before eating.*

Shaved Cauliflower Salad
with Lemon Vinaigrette and Parm

Serves 4 to 6 | Prep Time: 20 minutes | Total Time: 20 minutes

Some children grew up with fruit plates as a snack; I grew up with crisp, salted cauliflower to nibble on. My mom would always buy a bigger cauliflower than needed for a recipe, since we'd munch on pretty much half of it before cooking. Heavily inspired by my mother's cauliflower snacking plates, this simple shaved cauliflower tossed in a lemon vinaigrette was born.

In a world where cauliflower seems to get relegated to replacing one carb or another, there's something refreshing in letting cauliflower be its true self. Thinly shaved to highlight its pleasant crunch, the cauliflower may have a modest flavor, but it's perfectly paired with the punchy vinaigrette in this chic, monochromatic salad.

3 tablespoons extra-virgin olive oil, plus more for serving

1 teaspoon grated lemon zest

3 tablespoons fresh lemon juice, plus more to taste

3 garlic cloves, minced

Kosher salt and freshly ground black pepper

1 medium head cauliflower (about 2½ pounds)

⅓ cup shaved Parmesan cheese (see Note)

In a large bowl, whisk together the olive oil, lemon zest, lemon juice, garlic, a big pinch of salt, and lots of black pepper. Taste and adjust the salt and acid as needed.

Slice the cauliflower head into 4 wedges. Using a mandoline and working over the bowl with the dressing, shave the cauliflower into ¼-inch slices. (If you don't own a mandoline, you can use a sharp knife instead.) The cauliflower will break up a little bit as you shave, dropping tiny florets and crumbs as you go; you can reposition the cauliflower wedge on the mandoline as you go, but don't stress if not every slice is perfect. Toss and coat the cauliflower slices in the dressing.

Transfer the dressed cauliflower to a serving platter and top with the shaved Parmesan. Top with more olive oil, lemon juice, and black pepper and serve.

Note: *To keep things dairy-free, you can skip the Parm and finely grate some walnuts all over. Their buttery, nutty flavor brings a whole new dimension to the salad.*

Fennel Caesar Salad
with Garlic Lemon Panko

Serves 2 to 4 | Prep Time: 25 minutes | Cook Time: 5 minutes | Total Time: 30 minutes

Romaine lettuce isn't the only thing that deserves to get doused in a silky Caesar dressing. I love pairing this classic dressing with bolder vegetables, such as raw fennel. To me, the best parts about fennel are its crisp texture and peppery notes. Soak the finely shaved fennel in an ice bath to bring out its ultimate crunch potential, then toss in the creamy dressing. Something you should absolutely not skip? The crunchy panko. It replaces Caesar salad croutons with an evenly distributed layer of crunch in every bite.

Garlic Lemon Panko

2 tablespoons extra-virgin olive oil

2 garlic cloves, minced or grated

1 teaspoon grated lemon zest

⅓ cup panko or other bread crumbs

Kosher salt

Fennel Caesar Salad

1 large or 2 small fennel bulbs, very thinly sliced, wispy fronds reserved for serving

4 anchovy fillets in oil, chopped or crushed with a fork

1 large egg yolk

2 garlic cloves, finely grated or minced

Grated zest of ½ lemon

2 tablespoons fresh lemon juice

1 teaspoon Dijon mustard

⅓ cup neutral oil, such as sunflower or grapeseed

¼ cup finely grated Parmesan cheese

Kosher salt

Shaved Parmesan cheese, for serving

Make the garlic lemon panko: In a small skillet, heat the olive oil over medium heat. Add the garlic and lemon zest and cook until fragrant, about 1 minute. Add the panko and a pinch of salt and cook, stirring constantly, until golden and crispy. Transfer the crispy bread crumbs to a plate to cool.

Make the fennel Caesar salad: Fill a medium bowl with cold water and a few handfuls of ice. Add the sliced fennel and set aside to crisp up.

In a medium bowl, whisk together the anchovies, egg yolk, garlic, lemon zest, lemon juice, and mustard. Whisking constantly, slowly stream in the oil, just a few drops at a time at first. Whisk until smooth and emulsified. Add the grated Parmesan and whisk once more to combine. Taste and adjust the salt as needed (the anchovies are pretty salty, so you may not need much here).

Drain the fennel and dry thoroughly using a clean kitchen towel or salad spinner. Add the fennel to the dressing bowl and toss well to coat.

Arrange the dressed fennel on a serving plate. Scatter the crunchy panko and shaved Parmesan all over, and top with the reserved fennel fronds. Serve right away.

Notes:

• *If the dressing breaks because you've added too much oil at once, add a second egg yolk or a teaspoon of mustard to a clean bowl. Slowly stream the broken dressing in the bowl, vigorously whisking to emulsify.*

• *If you can't get behind anchovies, use 2 or 3 teaspoons of soy sauce or white miso to replicate that umami/saltiness.*

Toasted Farro Apple Salad
with Pecans and Maple Dressing

Serves 4 to 6 | Prep Time: 20 minutes | Cook Time: 40 minutes | Total Time: 1 hour

This seriously filling salad has the feel of something you'd make after an all-day apple picking session. It's a celebration of autumn, packed with crisp tart apples, chewy earthy farro, plus peppery arugula. The maple syrup, cumin, and cinnamon coat the salad in warmth and flavor.

Whenever I eat farro, I'm reminded of going fishing with my neighbors when we were five or six years old. Our mothers would boil a bunch of farro for us to use as fish bait, but we'd end up snacking on half of it by the time we made our way to the lake! Although I haven't gone fishing since then, I haven't stopped snacking on farro.

¼ cup plus 1 tablespoon extra-virgin olive oil

1 cup pearled farro

Kosher salt

1½ cups chopped pecans

1 teaspoon cumin seeds

¼ teaspoon ground cinnamon

¼ cup apple cider vinegar, plus more to taste

3 tablespoons maple syrup, plus more to taste

1 tablespoon Dijon mustard

2 medium Honeycrisp or Pink Lady apples (about 1 pound), cut into ½-inch cubes

2 cups packed baby arugula, chopped

In a medium saucepan, heat 1 tablespoon of the oil over medium heat. Add the farro and cook, stirring occasionally, until fragrant and toasty, about 3 minutes. Add 3 cups water and a big pinch of salt and bring to a boil. Cook the farro, stirring occasionally, until fully cooked through and tender, 20 to 30 minutes. Drain the farro and set aside to cool.

Preheat the oven to 400°F. Line a baking sheet with parchment paper.

Spread the pecans, cumin seeds, and cinnamon on the baking sheet and toss to combine. Bake until the spiced pecans are fragrant, 6 to 10 minutes. Let cool on the pan.

In a medium bowl, combine the vinegar, maple syrup, mustard, and a pinch of salt and whisk to combine. Whisking constantly, slowly add the remaining ¼ cup olive oil to emulsify. Taste and adjust the seasoning, adding more salt, vinegar, or maple syrup as needed.

In a large bowl, combine the cooked farro, toasted pecans and spices, apples, arugula, and the dressing and toss to coat. Serve right away.

Cucumber Salad
with Salted Lemon Yogurt

Serves 4 | Prep Time: 10 minutes | Total Time: 10 minutes

This creamy cucumber salad recipe tastes like refreshing dollops of tzatziki but with a lot more crunch and bite for my fellow texture-seekers. Instead of the grated, squeezed cucumber you'll commonly find in the delicious Greek sauce, my recipe uses salted crunchy, chunky cucumber slices. Pile them over garlicky yogurt swirled on a colorful platter. For some extra zing, I like to shower the cucumbers with lemon zest, then go in with freshly squeezed lemon juice and Calabrian chiles for a pleasant kick.

1 pound Persian (mini) cucumbers, cut into ¼-inch slices

Kosher salt

1 cup whole-milk Greek yogurt

3 garlic cloves, grated or minced

½ teaspoon grated lemon zest, plus more for serving

4 tablespoons fresh lemon juice, plus more to taste

3 tablespoons extra-virgin olive oil

2 tablespoons finely chopped fresh dill

1 small Calabrian or red Fresno chile, finely chopped (optional)

In a medium bowl, combine the cucumbers and a hefty pinch of salt. Using your hands, toss and gently squeeze the cucumber slices, crushing some of them.

In a small bowl, whisk together the yogurt, garlic, lemon zest, 1 tablespoon of the lemon juice, and a pinch of salt. Spread the garlic yogurt on a serving plate or platter.

To the bowl with the cucumbers, add the olive oil, remaining 3 tablespoons lemon juice, and the dill and toss to combine. Taste and season with more salt or lemon juice as needed.

Pile the cucumbers right in the middle of the yogurt, pouring the juices from the bowl all over the cucumbers and yogurt. Top the salad with more lemon zest and the chopped chiles (if using).

Evergreen Potato Salad

Serves 6 | Prep Time: 25 minutes, plus 2 hours chilling | Cook Time: 20 minutes |
Total Time: 2 hours 45 minutes

If there's something you'll find lots of in this book, it's potato recipes. Potatoes are one of my favorite sides, so I made sure to include a variety of starchy dishes like a gratin, roasted potatoes, sweet potatoes, and not one, but two potato salads. This bright, creamy version is heavily packed with fresh herbs, the perfect way to welcome warmer weather. It's one of the first things I make when spring pops around the corner and the local markets start carrying all the fresh green herbs, crunchy sugar snap peas, and crisp scallions—what an exciting time!

Kosher salt

1½ to 2 pounds baby Yukon Gold
    potatoes

¼ cup extra-virgin olive oil

¼ cup finely chopped fresh dill

¼ cup finely chopped fresh
    cilantro

¼ cup finely chopped fresh
    parsley

4 scallions, thinly sliced

2 tablespoons rice vinegar

1 small shallot, finely chopped

2 garlic cloves, grated or minced

¾ cup mayonnaise

2 cups sugar snap peas,
    sliced in half

Bring a large saucepan of water to a boil over medium-high heat. Season with a big pinch of salt and add the potatoes. Boil, stirring occasionally, until the potatoes are fork-tender, 20 to 25 minutes. Drain and set the potatoes aside to cool.

In a medium bowl, combine the olive oil, dill, cilantro, parsley, scallions, vinegar, shallot, and garlic, plus a hefty pinch of salt.

In a large bowl, whisk together the mayo and a heaping ½ cup of the herb mixture. Set both bowls aside.

Using a paring knife or just your fingers, peel the potatoes—their skins should slip off pretty easily. Add the peeled potatoes to the large bowl with the mayo mixture, breaking up any larger potatoes as you go. Add the snap peas and toss well to coat.

Cover and refrigerate for at least 2 hours and up to overnight.

When it's time to serve, arrange the potato salad on a wide plate and dollop the remaining herb mixture on top. Serve right away.

Notes:

• *If you see an herb you're not a fan of, switch it up for something more inviting. Not a fan of cilantro? Add some extra parsley. Do you absolutely despise fresh dill? Try chives instead.*

• *Removing the potato skins will be so worth it: It guarantees a buttery, tender mouthfeel while allowing the potatoes to absorb more of the dressing's flavors. You can always roast the peels with a little olive oil and salt for a fun snack or topping. That said, the recipe will absolutely work with unpeeled potatoes.*

• *But if you really don't feel like peeling a bunch of tiny potatoes, you can use larger Yukon Gold potatoes, boil them, peel them, then slice them into bite-size pieces.*

Crisp Green Salad
with Caramelized Citrus Dressing

Serves 4 to 6 | Prep Time: 15 minutes | Cook Time: 20 minutes | Total Time: 35 minutes

We all need a reliable yet impressive green salad recipe we can whip up for any occasion and know it's going to be a crowd-pleaser. The trick to making a fantastic green salad starts with the dressing, and in this case, a caramelized citrus version made with sugar-coated roasted citrus slices—sweet, earthy, and tart. They get finely chopped and mixed with lemon juice, honey, and good-quality olive oil for a sleek and complex vinaigrette that will turn any mundane lettuce leaf into a memorable one.

1 small orange, such as Cara Cara or navel, cut into ½-inch slices, ends reserved

1 small Meyer or regular lemon (see page 21), cut into ½-inch slices, ends reserved

¼ cup extra-virgin olive oil

2 tablespoons sugar

2 heads Little Gem or romaine lettuce, root ends trimmed, leaves separated

2 tablespoons fresh lemon juice, plus more to taste

2 tablespoons honey

1 teaspoon rice vinegar

½ teaspoon grated fresh ginger (optional)

Kosher salt

⅓ cup coarsely chopped pistachios

⅓ cup shaved aged cheese, such as Gruyère, sharp cheddar, or Parmesan (see Note)

Flaky salt, for serving

Preheat the oven to 400°F.

Arrange the orange and Meyer lemon slices on a small baking sheet or quarter-baking sheet. Drizzle with the olive oil and sprinkle the sugar all over.

Roast until the citrus is softened and beginning to caramelize, 14 to 16 minutes.

Preheat the broiler. Place the oven rack about 4 inches from the heating element. Broil the citrus for 2 to 4 minutes, watching closely, until the flesh develops a brown, sizzling crust. Carefully transfer the roasted citrus to a cutting board to cool.

Use the cut sides of the reserved citrus ends to help you "scrub" any browned bits from the baking sheet, adding the browned bits and the residual oil to a medium bowl. Discard the citrus ends.

In a large bowl of ice water, add the lettuce leaves and let sit to crisp up while you make the dressing.

Finely chop the cooled roasted citrus and add it to the bowl with the oil and browned bits. Add the lemon juice, honey, vinegar, ginger (if using), and a pinch of kosher salt and whisk to combine. The dressing should be the consistency of a loose, spoonable jam. Taste and adjust the salt or acid as needed. If the dressing seems too thick, you can loosen it with a splash of cold water.

Drain the lettuce and dry using a clean kitchen towel or salad spinner.

In a large bowl, toss the lettuce with half of the dressing to coat.

To serve, add the dressed lettuce to a large serving platter in an even layer. Spoon over the remaining dressing and top with the chopped pistachios, shaved cheese, and flaky salt.

Note: *If you want to keep this dairy-free, skip the cheese shavings and finely grate some cashews or walnuts on top.*

Broccoli Sweet Potato Harvest Salad
with Maple Sesame Crunch

Serves 4 to 6 | Prep Time: 25 minutes | Cook Time: 35 minutes | Total Time: 1 hour

A recipe to celebrate the fall harvest season: Roasted broccoli, crunchy kale, and sweet potatoes are dressed in a mustard maple vinaigrette and topped with feta chunks. The best part about this recipe? The maple sesame crunch! I will often make an extra batch, just to snack on as I'm prepping the actual salad. It's sweet, toasty, and adds a lovely texture to every bite. Since the salad feeds a crowd, you can assemble it a few hours ahead of time, keeping the sesame bark separate and crumbling it on top right before serving to keep it nice and crunchy.

Salted Maple Sesame Bark

½ cup sesame seeds

2 tablespoons maple syrup

1 tablespoon neutral oil, such as sunflower or grapeseed

½ teaspoon kosher salt

Harvest Salad

2 medium bunches lacinato or green curly kale

1 medium head broccoli, stalk peeled and thinly sliced, broken into florets

1 medium sweet potato, peeled and sliced into ¼-inch-thick rounds

¼ cup neutral oil, such as sunflower or grapeseed

Boiling water

Salt

Maple Dijon Dressing

3 tablespoons maple syrup

3 tablespoons rice vinegar or apple cider vinegar, plus more to taste

3 tablespoons extra-virgin olive oil, plus more to taste

2 tablespoons Dijon mustard

3 garlic cloves, minced or grated

Kosher salt

Assembly

Kosher salt

¾ cup crumbled feta cheese

Make the salted maple sesame bark: Preheat the oven to 400°F. Line a baking sheet with parchment paper.

In a small bowl, stir together the sesame seeds, maple syrup, oil, and salt. Pour the sesame mixture onto the baking sheet and spread it into an even layer, aiming for about ¼-inch thickness. Bake until fragrant and toasty, 10 to 12 minutes. Set aside to cool completely.

Make the harvest salad: Increase the oven temperature to 425°F. Line two baking sheets with parchment paper.

Strip the kale leaves off the stems, separating the leaves and stems into two different piles. Finely chop the kale leaves and add them to a colander.

Finely chop the kale stems. Cut any larger broccoli florets into bite-size pieces. Evenly arrange the chopped kale stems, broccoli florets, sliced broccoli stalk, and sliced sweet potato on the two baking sheets. Drizzle the oil all over and season with a big pinch of salt. Toss well to coat.

Roast for 20 minutes. Preheat the broiler. Place the oven rack about 4 inches from the heating element. Broil the vegetables, keeping a close eye on them, until they're nicely charred in some places, 2 to 3 minutes.

Set the colander full of kale leaves in the sink or over a large bowl. Pour a few cups of boiling water all over the kale leaves to wilt them (this makes them easier to chew) and drain. Rinse the kale under cold water and squeeze any remaining water from the kale with your hands.

Make the maple Dijon dressing: In a medium bowl, whisk together the maple syrup, vinegar, oil, mustard, garlic, and a pinch of salt. Taste and adjust the seasoning, adding more salt, oil, or vinegar as needed.

Assemble the salad: In a large bowl, add the kale leaves, a pinch of salt, and about half of the dressing. Massage the mixture with your hands for a minute or two to let the dressing penetrate the kale. Add the roasted vegetables and feta and toss again. Drizzle the remaining dressing over the top and crumble the crunchy sesame bark all over. Serve right away.

Afghan-Inspired Carrot Raisin Salad

Serves 4 | Prep Time: 10 minutes, plus 2 hours chilling | Cook Time: 20 minutes |
Total Time: 2 hours 30 minutes

Carrots? Not my favorite. Raisins? Not a huge fan of those, either. This salad? I could eat it all in one sitting. I was introduced to this salad at an Afghan restaurant while trying their Kabuli pulao. While the carrots and raisins are commonly dolloped on top of or mixed in the dish, they served a carrot-raisin side salad— mind-blowing. This sweet carrot-raisin slaw was so memorable, I spent the following weeks re-creating it. I learned a store-bought bag of shredded carrots will have the best texture. My version is a touch brighter due to the addition of the not-so-traditional lime juice, which contrasts all that warm sweetness. Serve it with Chicken Schnitzel (page 81) or Lemon Pepper Roast Chicken (page 87).

½ cup plus 2 tablespoons light or dark brown sugar

¼ cup raisins, chopped

2 teaspoons kosher salt, plus more to taste

1¼ teaspoons ground green cardamom

1 (10-ounce) bag shredded or julienned carrots

¼ cup fresh lime juice, plus lime wedges for squeezing

In a medium saucepan, combine ½ cup of the brown sugar, the raisins, salt, 1 teaspoon of the cardamom, and 4 cups water. Bring to a boil over medium heat. Reduce the heat to medium-low and simmer until the brown sugar has fully dissolved and the mixture is very fragrant, about 10 minutes. Add the carrots and cook until tender and easy to chew, 10 to 12 minutes.

Set a fine-mesh strainer or colander over a large bowl. Drain the carrots, reserving the liquid in the bowl (see Note).

Transfer the drained carrots to a medium bowl. Add the lime juice, the remaining 2 tablespoons brown sugar, the remaining ¼ teaspoon cardamom, a small pinch of salt, and ¼ cup of the reserved cooking liquid. Toss well to combine. Cover and refrigerate for at least 2 hours and up to overnight. Check for seasoning once more (since cooler temperatures can dull flavor), adding salt if needed.

Serve chilled with lime wedges on the side.

Note: *The simmering broth tastes like liquid carrot cake! You can drink it as a hot tea, chill it and top it off with ice and seltzer, or add it to your favorite cocktail.*

side
dish
savvy

Potato-Leek Gratin

Serves 6 to 8 | Prep Time: 30 minutes | Cook Time: 1 hour 45 minutes | Total Time: 2 hours 15 minutes

We all need a reliable, showstopping side dish ready to impress our guests, and this potato-leek gratin is a great contender for that role. I like describing this recipe as an elevated classic: You'll find the typical flavors of a potato gratin, with some extra zhuzh to balance its richness. I'm talking about fragrant lemon zest, floral coriander, a homemade buttermilk mix made with cream and vinegar for some pleasant acidity, and sweet melted leeks.

8 tablespoons (4 ounces) unsalted butter, plus more for greasing

2 pounds Yukon Gold potatoes

6 medium leeks

Kosher salt

2 teaspoons grated lemon zest

2 teaspoons ground coriander

2 teaspoons freshly ground black pepper

2 teaspoons minced fresh rosemary leaves

1½ cups heavy cream

2 tablespoons distilled white or apple cider vinegar

4 ounces Gruyère or sharp cheddar cheese, coarsely grated

Note: *The best part about this dish may or may not be the leftovers. I love making this recipe, since I know my breakfast will be sorted for a few days. Here's what you do: Add the gratin to a pan over medium heat and crisp it up until the potatoes start developing a beautifully golden crust. Crack a couple of eggs around the potatoes, cover, and steam until the egg white is cooked through. Serve right away, smearing the runny yolks all over the crunchy, warm gratin.*

Preheat the oven to 400°F. Lightly grease a 9 × 13-inch baking dish with butter.

Fill a large bowl about halfway with cold water. Using a mandoline or a sharp knife, very thinly slice the potatoes (about ⅛-inch slices). Add the sliced potatoes to the cold water.

Fill a second large bowl with cold water. Trim off the leek roots and dark green leaves (freeze them and use them for making stock). Remove the outer layer of each leek. Slice the white and light-green parts into coins ½ inch thick. You should be left with 7 to 8 cups of sliced leeks. Add the leeks to the water and thoroughly rinse them to get rid of any dirt in between layers. Drain the leeks and rinse them again while moving them around in the fine-mesh strainer.

In a large sauté pan, melt 7 tablespoons of the butter over medium heat. Add the leeks and a good pinch of salt and cook, stirring occasionally, until they're a deep golden color and quite soft, about 10 minutes. If the leeks are browning too fast, reduce the heat as needed.

Reduce the heat to medium-low. Move the leeks to the sides of the pan and add the remaining 1 tablespoon butter to the center. Once it's melted, add the lemon zest, coriander, black pepper, and rosemary and fry them in the butter until fragrant and golden, about 2 minutes. Add the cream and vinegar, plus another big pinch of salt, and stir to combine. Remove the pan from the heat.

Drain the sliced potatoes well and transfer them to the baking dish. Pour the creamy leek mixture over the potatoes and sprinkle the cheese all over. Using a spatula, carefully toss the mixture to combine and coat the potato slices evenly. You can help the potatoes get re-nestled with the spatula but no need to overthink it. Some nice craggy bits are good. Tightly cover the pan with aluminum foil.

Bake until the potatoes are very tender, about 1 hour. Carefully remove the foil and return the pan to the oven and bake until the top and edges develop a deep golden crust, another 25 to 30 minutes.

Let cool for about 10 minutes and serve hot.

Steamy Roasted Cabbage
with Crispy Garlic Pistachio Oil

Serves 4 | Prep Time: 10 minutes | Cook Time: 35 minutes | Total Time: 45 minutes

Cabbage is probably in my top five favorite vegetables—it's so versatile and I can't get enough of it. It can be fermented and turned into tangy sauerkraut, rolled into meaty cabbage rolls, transformed into a creamy coleslaw, but my favorite way of preparing it, by far, is roasting it at a high temperature, heavily drenched in olive oil. The sides get caramelized, the interior softens just like butter, and it simply melts in your mouth. You can keep the cabbage wedges as they are or level it up with a garlicky pistachio topping, infused with coriander and punchy black pepper. The topping falls in between the cabbage leaves, filling all of its nooks and crannies, while the garlic oil floods the center.

    This showstopper side dish goes perfectly with grilled fish, roasted chicken, or a medium-rare steak.

Roasted Cabbage

1 small head green cabbage (about 2 pounds)

¼ cup extra-virgin olive oil

Kosher salt

Pistachio Garlic Oil Topping

½ teaspoon black peppercorns

½ teaspoon coriander seeds

½ cup neutral oil, such as sunflower or grapeseed

12 garlic cloves, thinly sliced

1 teaspoon grated lemon zest

¼ cup pistachios, finely chopped

2 teaspoons fresh lemon juice, plus more to taste

Kosher salt

Make the roasted cabbage: Preheat the oven to 425°F. Line a baking sheet with parchment paper.

Cut the cabbage in half through the core. Slice each half of cabbage into 3 wedges through the core. Arrange the cabbage wedges on the baking sheet and drizzle the olive oil all over. Flip the cabbage to evenly coat it in the oil and season with a big pinch of salt.

Roast until the undersides of the cabbage edges have browned a bit and start to char, about 20 minutes. Using tongs or a spatula, flip the cabbage wedges. Continue roasting until the cabbage is soft and steamy inside and charred and crisp on the edges, 10 to 15 minutes.

Make the pistachio garlic oil topping: In a mortar and pestle, crush the peppercorns and coriander seeds lightly. (You can also do this by putting the spices in between layers of paper towel and going over them a few times with a rolling pin.)

In a small skillet, combine the oil and the garlic and cook over medium-low heat until the garlic is lightly golden and starts to look crispy, 6 to 7 minutes. Remove the pan from the heat. Add the crushed black pepper/coriander mix, plus the lemon zest and stir to combine. Add the pistachios, lemon juice, and a pinch of salt and stir again. Taste and adjust the seasoning with more salt or lemon juice as needed.

Arrange the roasted cabbage on a serving plate and dollop the topping all over. Serve hot.

Lemon Lover's Turmeric-Roasted Potatoes

Serves 4 | Prep Time: 15 minutes | Cook Time: 1 hour 25 minutes | Total Time: 1 hour 40 minutes

I'd like to introduce you to my take on deliciously tart Greek lemon potatoes: With the addition of turmeric, these tender, ultra-tangy, lemony potatoes develop a bright yellow color and an inviting earthy flavor, the perfect accompaniment to any savory protein. This is a one-pan recipe that starts with a turmeric-lemon marinade. The potatoes absorb all of that flavor and liquid in the oven, developing crispy, crunchy edges and a tender, melt-in-your-mouth interior. I like serving them over a bed of rich, cold sour cream and showering them with fresh dill.

½ cup fresh lemon juice (about 3 lemons)

¼ cup extra-virgin olive oil

4 garlic cloves, smashed

1 teaspoon ground turmeric

2 pounds Yukon Gold potatoes, unpeeled, cut into 1-inch cubes

Kosher salt and freshly ground black pepper

2 teaspoons grated lemon zest

1 cup sour cream (see Note)

Chopped fresh dill, for serving

Preheat the oven to 425°F.

In a 9 × 13-inch roasting pan (see Note), combine the lemon juice, ½ cup water, olive oil, garlic, and turmeric. Add the potatoes, season liberally with salt and pepper, and tightly cover the pan with foil, wrapping it around the edges of the pan.

Roast until the potatoes have absorbed most of the liquid in the pan (there might be a little liquid left) and have a vibrant yellow color, 40 to 45 minutes.

Carefully remove the foil and toss the potatoes in the remaining juices. Roast until the potatoes are softened with a few crispy edges, 35 to 40 more minutes.

Toss the potatoes with the lemon zest. Spread the sour cream on a serving platter and add the potatoes in the middle. Sprinkle with the fresh dill and serve immediately.

Notes:

• *If you want to keep this side dish dairy-free, skip the sour cream and finish off the roasted potatoes with a drizzle of olive oil on top.*

• *A sweet little warning: Whatever you do, don't use your grandmother's heirloom baking dish or that unique vintage baking pan you spent way too much money on at a flea market to bake these potatoes in. The concentrated turmeric marinade may or may not stain the vessel. Try using something a little less precious—while I was developing this recipe, my enameled baking dish made it out spotless, while my $6 baking pan came out with a couple of ridiculously yellow battle scars.*

Crispy Smashed Potatoes
with Sour Cream and Charred Scallions

Serves 4 to 6 | Prep Time: 20 minutes | Cook Time: 50 minutes | Total Time: 1 hour 10 minutes

These potatoes taste like a bag of sour cream & onion chips that have matured into a sophisticated grown-up. And as is true of a good bag of chips, it'll be hard to stop eating crunchy smashed potatoes with soft, buttery flesh that get topped with dollops of sour cream and smoky charred scallions.

Charring is such a simple, no-fuss technique that helps us add multiple dimensions to a single ingredient: Some parts of the scallions keep their peppery freshness, some get richer and smokier in flavor.

Smashed Potatoes

3 pounds baby Yukon Gold potatoes (28 to 30 small potatoes)

¼ cup kosher salt, plus more for sprinkling

¼ cup extra-virgin olive oil, plus more for drizzling

Charred Scallion Topping

15 scallions

1 teaspoon freshly crushed coriander seeds

1 teaspoon freshly crushed black pepper

¼ cup extra-virgin olive oil

2 garlic cloves, minced or finely grated

Grated zest of ½ lime

1 teaspoon fresh lime juice

Kosher salt

1 cup sour cream, plus more to taste

Flaky salt, for serving

Make the smashed potatoes: Preheat the oven to 425°F. Line one large or two standard baking sheets with parchment paper.

In a large pot, combine the potatoes, kosher salt, and 6 cups water. Bring to a boil and cook until the potatoes are tender and easily pierced with a fork, 7 to 10 minutes. Remove from the heat and drain.

Transfer the potatoes to the baking sheet(s) and toss well with the olive oil. Arrange them in a single even layer. Use a flat-bottomed glass to press each potato down just enough to smash it, but not completely crumble it. (Some potatoes will inevitably crumble into a bunch of pieces, but that's totally fine.) Drizzle a bit more oil all over the potatoes and sprinkle with a big pinch of salt.

Roast until the potatoes begin to crisp and sizzle around the edges, about 20 minutes. Flip the potatoes and continue roasting until crispy and browned all over, 15 to 20 minutes.

Meanwhile, make the charred scallion topping: Trim the root ends of the scallions. Heat a large dry cast-iron skillet over medium heat for 5 minutes or until nearly smoking. Add the scallions to the pan and arrange them in an even layer. Weight them down using a grill weight or another skillet to increase the contact surface for charring. Sear the scallions until they're smoky, fragrant, and well-charred in some places, 3 to 4 minutes. Use a pair of tongs to flip the scallions and cook until they're crisp in some places and softened in others, another 3 to 4 minutes. Remove the pan from the heat and transfer the scallions to a cutting board to cool slightly.

Add the crushed coriander and black pepper to the pan, still off the heat, and toast in the residual heat until fragrant, 1 or 2 minutes. Add the spices to a medium bowl to cool.

Chop the scallions into ½-inch pieces and add them to the bowl. Add the olive oil, garlic, lime zest, lime juice, and a pinch of salt and stir to combine. Taste and adjust the seasoning.

Arrange the roasted smashed potatoes on a serving platter. Spoon small dollops of sour cream on top and the scallion mixture all over the potatoes. Finish with flaky salt and serve.

Honey Balsamic Roasted Cauliflower

Serves 4 | Prep Time: 15 minutes | Cook Time: 45 minutes | Total Time: 1 hour

Don't we all need a reliable, easy side dish recipe we can pull out of our pocket anytime? I've got a roasted cauliflower recipe just for you. It all starts with a honey balsamic vinaigrette—that's delicious enough to toss a salad in—that we use to coat the cauliflower florets before we roast them until tender, crisp, and charred in certain spots, caramelized in others.

This recipe is so versatile: You can add the honey balsamic cauliflower to a dinner bowl or a sandwich, use it as a side dish to any hearty meat, or fry it with a couple of eggs the next morning.

¼ cup balsamic vinegar, plus more to taste

3 tablespoons honey

1 tablespoon Dijon mustard

3 garlic cloves, finely grated or minced

Kosher salt

¼ cup extra-virgin olive oil, plus more to taste

1 medium head cauliflower (1½ to 2 pounds)

Preheat the oven to 425°F. Line a baking sheet with parchment paper.

In a large bowl, whisk together the balsamic vinegar, honey, and mustard until all of the honey has dissolved into the mixture. Add the garlic and a pinch of salt and whisk again. Constantly whisk as you slowly stream in the olive oil, whisking until emulsified. Taste and adjust the seasoning, adding more salt, oil, or balsamic vinegar as needed.

Break off any leaves from the cauliflower. (Save them for a stir-fry, they're delicious.) Slice the cauliflower in half through the core. Break off the florets, slicing any larger ones in half. Slice the cauliflower stem into ¼-inch pieces.

Add all the cauliflower to the bowl. Toss well to coat, gently massaging the dressing into the cracks of the florets. Arrange the cauliflower cut-side down on the baking sheet, in an even layer.

Roast until tender and charred at the edges, 40 to 45 minutes. Serve right away.

Roasted Broccoli
with Creamy Cheddar Sauce and Buttery Panko

Serves 4 to 6 | Prep Time: 20 minutes | Cook Time: 40 minutes | Total Time: 1 hour

When you think of a vegetarian main, a whole head of broccoli might not come up as a potential contender, but it was one of my mother's go-tos when I was growing up. Whenever she'd run out of meat to thaw or she wanted a lighter meal, she would boil a couple of whole heads of broccoli, stems and all, then drench them in a steamy, just-made béchamel sauce. Served with fresh salad on the side, the béchamel-covered broccoli would always be a hit.

My broccoli side dish recipe takes inspiration from that comforting meal I so dearly enjoyed as a kid. Instead of boiling the broccoli, I like to roast it. If boiling the broccoli softens the fibers, roasting it leads to significantly more flavor development. The pleasantly earthy and slightly bitter roasted broccoli will be ready to absorb all the richness of the sharp cheddar sauce. For extra texture, you can't go wrong with lightly toasted, buttery panko.

Roasted Broccoli

2 pounds broccoli (about 2 medium heads)

⅓ cup extra-virgin olive oil

Kosher salt

Buttery Panko

2 tablespoons unsalted butter

½ cup panko or other bread crumbs

Kosher salt

Cheddar Béchamel

2 tablespoons unsalted butter

2 tablespoons all-purpose flour

1 garlic clove, finely chopped

1½ cups whole milk

Kosher salt

5 ounces sharp cheddar cheese, finely grated

Make the roasted broccoli: Preheat the oven to 425°F. Line a baking sheet with parchment paper.

Break the top part of the broccoli into large florets. Using a vegetable peeler, peel the broccoli stalk and slice it into roughly ¼-inch pieces. Add the sliced stalk pieces to the baking sheet. Slice the large florets in half, through the stalk, and add them to the baking sheet. Drizzle with the oil and season with a big pinch of salt. Toss well to coat and arrange the florets cut-side down on the pan.

Roast the broccoli until charred on the edges and softened throughout, 30 to 35 minutes.

Meanwhile, make the buttery panko: In a medium saucepan, melt the butter over medium heat until hot and foamy. Add the panko and a pinch of salt and cook, stirring frequently, until the bread crumbs have absorbed the butter and are golden brown, about 5 minutes. Transfer the bread crumbs to a plate.

Make the cheddar béchamel: Return the saucepan to medium heat (no need to wipe it out) and melt the butter. Add the flour and whisk until the flour is golden and smells toasty, 2 to 3 minutes. Add the garlic and cook until fragrant, about 1 minute. Whisking constantly, slowly add the milk. Continue cooking and whisking until thickened, 4 to 5 minutes. Add a pinch of salt and whisk to combine. Remove the pan from the heat.

Add the cheese to the sauce and fold it in with a silicone spatula. The residual heat will melt and emulsify the cheese into the sauce.

Pile the roasted broccoli on a serving plate. Pour the sauce all over the broccoli and scatter the crunchy panko on top. Serve hot.

Roasted Squash
with Pepita Pesto

Serves 4 | Prep Time: 20 minutes | Cook Time: 40 minutes | Total Time: 1 hour

While I was growing up, my family would eat pumpkin once, maybe twice a year, roasted with a little bit of oil and salt. It was simple and delicious, but never exciting or something we'd look forward to. Moving to the US, I was incredibly surprised to see grocery stores and farmers' markets turn into pumpkin trading centers on the first day of September. You could walk in anywhere and get yourself the wildest pumpkin-based products, like pumpkin cheese, pumpkin soda, pumpkin soap, and pumpkin dog food. Since then, I've grown to enjoy pumpkin, especially as a side dish.

Inspired by the transitional period between late August and early September, when pumpkins and other squash are suddenly everywhere but your old faithful summer basil plant is on its last legs, this soft, custardy squash with nutty pepita pesto makes a memorable early fall dish.

Roasted Squash

2 small butternut squash or pumpkins (about 2 pounds total)

4 tablespoons extra-virgin olive oil

Kosher salt

Pepita Pesto

⅓ cup pepitas

1½ cups packed fresh basil leaves

3 garlic cloves

Kosher salt

½ cup finely grated Parmesan cheese

½ cup extra-virgin olive oil, plus more as needed

Flaky salt, for serving

Roast the squash: Preheat the oven to 425°F. Line two large baking sheets with parchment paper.

Peel the squash using a peeler. Trim off the stem and slice the squash in half, lengthwise. Using a spoon, scoop out the seeds (toss these in olive oil and spices and roast them later for snacking!). Using a sharp knife, slice the squash halves into ½-inch slices.

Divide the squash between the two baking sheets. Drizzle 2 tablespoons olive oil over each baking sheet and season with a big pinch of kosher salt. Toss everything to evenly coat and arrange the squash slices in an even layer.

Roast until the undersides are darkened and slightly crisp along the edges, about 20 minutes. Flip and continue roasting until the squash is caramelized and tender all the way through, another 15 to 20 minutes.

Meanwhile, make the pepita pesto: To a food processor, add the pepitas, the basil, the garlic, and a pinch of kosher salt. Pulse until the basil is broken down into small shreds. Add the Parmesan and olive oil and pulse again, being careful not to overprocess. Aim for a coarse, saucy pesto. (You can also do this in a mortar and pestle.) Taste and add more salt or olive oil if needed.

Arrange the roasted squash on a serving platter. Dollop the pesto all over the squash, finish with flaky salt, and serve right away.

Seared Summer Squash
with Soft Melting Lemons

Serves 4 | Prep Time: 15 minutes | Cook Time: 1 hour | Total Time: 1 hour 15 minutes

The late summer side dish to conquer them all: Summer squash gets halved and seared in a hot skillet to develop deeply flavorful char marks all over. Because you're working over high heat, the squash stays juicy, while a delicious crust is created on the outside. Meanwhile, you'll have your melting lemons going: Thinly shaved lemon slices are sealed in a parchment paper pocket and steam-baked. The lemons cook away in their own juices to give them a soft, tender texture and a concentrated lemon flavor that perfectly brightens up the charred zucchini.

2 medium Meyer or regular lemons (see page 21), thinly sliced

2 pounds small to medium summer squash, such as zucchini, yellow summer squash, lemon squash

¼ cup plus 2 tablespoons extra-virgin olive oil, plus more as needed

Kosher salt

1 garlic clove, finely grated

¼ cup packed fresh mint leaves, torn

Flaky salt

Preheat the oven to 400°F.

Pile the lemons in the center of a 9 × 12-inch sheet of aluminum foil or parchment paper. Lift two sides up to meet in the middle and fold them down to make a packet and tuck the two ends underneath. Set the pocket on a baking sheet.

Bake until the lemons steam and are super soft and melty, about 40 minutes.

Meanwhile, trim the ends off the squash and cut each squash in half lengthwise. Set the squash on a large baking sheet and drizzle with the ¼ cup of oil. Season with a big pinch of kosher salt and toss to coat.

Heat a large cast-iron skillet over medium-high heat until nearly smoking. Working in batches, place the squash cut-side down in the skillet, weighting it down using a grill press or another skillet. Sear until charred on the bottom and tender inside, 3 to 4 minutes. Flip the squash and cook for 2 to 3 minutes on the other side. Feel free to add a teaspoon of oil or so as needed if the pan seems dry or if the squash are sticking, and adjust the heat accordingly. Transfer the charred squash to a serving platter.

Carefully open the lemon packet and add the steamed lemons to the squash.

In a small bowl, combine the garlic and remaining 2 tablespoons of olive oil and drizzle on top of the squash. Toss the mint leaves all over the platter and sprinkle with flaky salt. Serve warm.

Note: *It's not in the ingredient list, but if you're feeling frisky, finish off the seared squash with a light drizzle of floral honey to complement all that smokiness and char.*

Roasted Sweet Potatoes
with Chile Brown Butter

Serves 4 to 6 | Prep Time: 15 minutes | Cook Time: 35 minutes | Total Time: 50 minutes

Tender sweet potatoes tossed in a spicy chile brown butter is a side dish you'll come back to again and again. While sweet potatoes are often made sweeter by adding maple syrup, brown sugar, or even marshmallows, this recipe keeps things deep and savory. To balance out the sweet, custardy flesh, the sweet potato rounds are paired with a nutty brown butter spiked with spicy but pleasantly bitter ground chiles, shallots, and caramelized tomato paste.

2½ to 3 pounds sweet potatoes, cut into ¾-inch-thick rounds

2 tablespoons neutral oil, such as sunflower or grapeseed

Kosher salt

4 tablespoons (2 ounces) unsalted butter

1 small shallot, finely chopped

1 teaspoon tomato paste

1 teaspoon Aleppo pepper or red chile flakes

½ teaspoon sweet paprika

¼ teaspoon cayenne pepper (optional)

Flaky salt, for serving

Fresh cilantro or parsley, for serving

Sour cream or Greek yogurt, for serving

Preheat the oven to 425°F. Line two baking sheets with parchment paper.

Add the sweet potatoes to the baking sheets, drizzle the oil all over, and season with a big pinch of kosher salt. Toss everything to evenly coat and arrange the sweet potatoes in an even layer. Roast until soft and tender, 30 to 35 minutes.

In a small skillet, melt the butter over medium heat, whisking occasionally, until you see golden brown specks in the bottom of the pan, 3 to 4 minutes. Add the shallot and tomato paste and cook, stirring frequently, until the shallot is fragrant and the tomato paste darkens, 2 to 3 minutes. Remove the pan from the heat. Add the Aleppo pepper, paprika, cayenne (if using), and a pinch of kosher salt and stir to combine.

Arrange the roasted sweet potato rounds on a large plate and pour the chile brown butter all over. Toss to coat and top with the flaky salt and cilantro. Serve warm with sour cream on the side.

Note: *If you're looking to make this dairy-free, skip the butter and use a nutty oil instead, such as sesame oil, hazelnut oil, or roasted peanut oil, and omit the sour cream.*

Melt-in-Your-Mouth Leeks
with Dijon Vinaigrette

Serves 2 to 4 | Prep Time: 15 minutes, plus 2 hours chilling | Cook Time: 40 minutes |
Total Time: 2 hours 55 minutes

Also known as poireaux vinaigrette, these meltingly tender leeks covered in a bright, tart vinaigrette and crunchy pistachios are a dream pairing for anything from roasted chicken to fried fish or even a hearty grilled steak. Gently poaching the leeks breaks down their cells and transforms the stalks into tender and delicate little gems. Here, I'm offering a base recipe that you can zhuzh on your own with different herbs, spices, or flavorful poaching liquids. Even better, you can make this dish ahead of time—just poach and chill the leeks and make the dressing, then assemble when it's time to serve.

4 medium leeks, root ends and
   dark green leaves trimmed

Kosher salt

1 tablespoon sugar

1 teaspoon black peppercorns

1 small shallot, thinly sliced

½ teaspoon finely grated
   lemon zest

1 tablespoon fresh lemon juice

1 teaspoon Dijon mustard

1½ tablespoons extra-virgin
   olive oil

2 tablespoons chopped fresh
   parsley leaves

2 tablespoons chopped roasted
   pistachios (salted or unsalted,
   either is okay)

Flaky salt, for serving

Remove the outer layer of each leek. This is usually where the most sand and silt get trapped, and this layer can sometimes get a little beat up on its journey to the store. Under cool running water, rinse the leeks, gently loosening some of the layers at the cut top to encourage the water to go through. Set the leeks aside.

In a medium skillet or pot, combine 2 tablespoons kosher salt, the sugar, peppercorns, and 2 cups water. Bring to a boil over medium heat. Carefully add the leeks and reduce the heat to low—you're looking for a very soft, gentle simmer with barely any bubbles. Poach the leeks until they can be easily pierced with a fork, 35 to 40 minutes.

Using a pair of tongs or a fork, transfer the leeks to a small plate (discard the poaching liquid). Refrigerate the leeks for at least 2 hours and up to overnight to chill.

Place the sliced shallot in a fine-mesh strainer and rinse under cold running water for 10 seconds or so. This will remove some of its pungency and leave you with a more delicate-tasting shallot. Set aside to continue draining.

In a medium bowl, whisk together the lemon zest, lemon juice, mustard, and a pinch of salt. While whisking, slowly stream in the oil, whisking until the mixture is smooth and emulsified.

Slice the cooled leeks into 1-inch coins and arrange them on a serving plate. (If some of the layers come off while cutting, just arrange them back together around the leek.) Spoon the vinaigrette all over the leeks and top with the shallots, fresh parsley, chopped pistachios, and flaky salt.

Honey Mustard Bok Choy

Serves 4 | Prep Time: 15 minutes | Cook Time: 5 minutes | Total Time: 20 minutes

Bok choy, a type of Chinese cabbage, is a cruciferous green vegetable that forms the base of this perfectly light side dish. You might be asking yourself, what could be so exciting about another green vegetable? When steamed, bok choy develops a ridiculously buttery taste and a soft, delicate feel, ready to take on our honey mustard emulsion. The honey mustard sauce is mild and not too overpowering, not too bitter, not too sweet.

You'll notice I'm sprinkling roughly crushed, toasted mustard seeds on the final dish. Now, you don't have to go out of your way to find them if you think you'll never use them again—though they're a must in homemade pickles and a great addition to any marinade, so I highly encourage you to try them out. Pair this wonderful side dish with roasted fish or a quickly seared steak.

1 tablespoon honey

2 teaspoons Dijon mustard

1 garlic clove, finely grated or minced

3 tablespoons neutral oil, such as sunflower or grapeseed

1 tablespoon fresh lemon juice

Kosher salt

½ teaspoon yellow mustard seeds

1 pound baby bok choy, sliced in half lengthwise and thoroughly rinsed

In a medium bowl, whisk together the honey, mustard, and garlic. Whisking constantly, slowly stream in the oil, just a few drops at a time at first. Whisk until smooth and emulsified. Add the lemon juice and a pinch of salt and whisk to combine.

In a small skillet, toast the mustard seeds over medium heat until fragrant and some of the seeds start to make a popping sound, about 1 minute. Remove the pan from the heat.

Transfer the toasted seeds to a mortar and pestle and crush them lightly. (You can also do this by putting the seeds between layers of paper towel and going over them a few times with a rolling pin.)

In a large saucepan, bring about 1 inch of water and a big pinch of salt to a boil over medium heat. Reduce the heat to medium-low, add the bok choy, cover, and steam for 2 minutes. Using tongs, flip the bok choy in the pan. Cover and steam until bright green, tender but still slightly crisp, about 2 minutes. Transfer the bok choy to a colander to drain.

Spread half of the honey mustard vinaigrette on a serving platter. Arrange the steamed bok choy right on top and drizzle the remaining vinaigrette all over. Sprinkle the toasted mustard seeds on top and serve right away.

Smoky and Sweet Marinated Peppers

Serves 4 | Prep Time: 10 minutes, plus 15 minutes chilling | Cook Time: 15 minutes | Total Time: 40 minutes

Smoky, plump, sweet marinated red peppers were a staple side dish in our kitchen while we were growing up. Although calling it a side dish might be a bit of a stretch, it's situated somewhere between a side dish and a condiment. Every time I make these, the smoky smell that fills up the room brings me back to helping my mother in the kitchen as a little girl. She'd cook these directly over our gas stove and get them ready for me to peel and toss in the marinade. We'd always keep them whole, stems on, and serve them next to hearty roasted chicken and mashed potatoes. They'd add the perfect level of acidity and brightness to any meal. If there were any leftovers, we'd throw them on a piece of toast topped with cheese and crispy fried eggs the next day.

1 pound mini sweet peppers or red piquillo peppers

¼ cup extra-virgin olive oil

¼ cup rice vinegar or apple cider vinegar, plus more to taste

2 tablespoons sugar

Kosher salt

Preheat the broiler. Place the oven rack about 4 inches from the heating element.

Place the peppers on a baking sheet. Broil until the tops of the peppers are blackened and flaky, 6 to 8 minutes. Using a pair of tongs, flip the peppers and broil until charred, another 5 to 7 minutes. Depending on the size of your peppers, you can repeat this until all sides are charred.

Transfer the charred peppers to a medium bowl and cover tightly with plastic wrap, a lid, or a plate and set aside until the peppers are still warm but comfortable to handle, about 15 minutes. The residual heat from the peppers will create steam and soften the skin, making them easier to peel.

Hold a pepper by the stem and carefully peel off the charred skin, keeping the stem attached. Add the skinned peppers and any residual juices to a medium bowl.

Add the olive oil, vinegar, sugar, and a big pinch of salt to the peppers and gently toss to coat. Taste and add more salt or vinegar as needed.

Serve right away or cover and refrigerate for up to 5 days.

Note: *This recipe easily doubles to feed a crowd or to keep extra peppers in the fridge to add to anything throughout the week.*

sweets & treats

Easy No-Bake Milk Chocolate Pie

Makes one 10-inch pie | Prep Time: 30 minutes, plus 3 hours chilling | Total Time: 3 hours 30 minutes

Milk chocolate doesn't get enough love, and this recipe is here to change that. This no-bake tangy chocolate pie is a perfect dessert in my book: highly shareable, easy to transport, and incredibly delicious. It starts with a crunchy chocolate cookie crust filled with a salted milk chocolate mousse. The sour cream tames the whipped cream's richness and adds a smooth mouthfeel and subtle tartness to every bite, while the salt brings out the sweetness of the chocolate. You don't have to stop here: add a dusting of malt powder to the mousse for a malted chocolate pie, or if mint-chocolate-chip ice cream is up your alley, flavor the mousse with a dash of peppermint extract and embrace the classic combo.

Cookie Crust

1 (14.3-ounce) package chocolate
   sandwich cookies (about
   36 cookies)

7 tablespoons (3½ oz/100g)
   unsalted butter, melted

¼ teaspoon (2g) kosher salt

Milk Chocolate Filling

8 ounces (240g) milk chocolate,
   chopped

1 cup (240g) heavy cream

½ teaspoon (3g) kosher salt

1 cup (240g) sour cream

For Serving

Flaky salt, for topping

Shaved or melted milk chocolate,
   for topping

Make the cookie crust: In a food processor, pulse the sandwich cookies until the mixture is mostly fine crumbs with small chunks of cookies here and there. Add the melted butter and salt and pulse to combine. (You can also do this step by adding the cookies to a large zip-seal bag and crushing them using a rolling pin until finely crumbled. Add the butter and kosher salt and mix to incorporate.)

Transfer the cookie mixture to a 10-inch pie dish. Use your hands or the bottom of a glass to press the mixture into an even layer covering the sides and bottom of the dish. Set the dish in the freezer while you make the filling.

Make the milk chocolate filling: In a small saucepan, bring 1 inch of water to a simmer. In a medium heatproof bowl, add the chocolate and place the bowl on top of the pan, trapping the steam. (Make sure the bottom of the bowl doesn't touch the water.) Using a small silicone spatula, stir the chocolate constantly as it melts. When about three-quarters of the chocolate has melted, remove the bowl and continue stirring until all of the chocolate is melted. (You can also melt the chocolate in 15-second spurts in the microwave if you're more comfortable with this.) Set the melted chocolate aside to cool to room temperature.

In a large bowl, and using an electric mixer (or in a bowl using just a whisk and your muscles), combine the cream and kosher salt. Whip the cream to soft peaks, about 3 minutes of constant whipping. Add the sour cream to the bowl and continue whipping until incorporated. Slowly stream in the cooled melted chocolate, whipping constantly, until all of the chocolate is incorporated and the mixture reaches stiff peaks.

Remove the pie crust from the freezer. Dollop the milk chocolate into the crust and evenly spread it using an offset or silicone spatula.

Refrigerate the pie for at least 3 hours before serving.

Top the pie with flaky salt and a little bit of melted or shaved chocolate. Slice and serve.

The Very Best Banana Bread

Makes one 8-inch loaf | Prep Time: 10 minutes | Cook Time: 1 hour | Total Time: 1 hour 10 minutes

In a world where everything is the best, I try saving my hyperboles for when I truly mean them. In this case, while it's a bold statement, I stand by it: This is the best banana bread I've ever had. It's one of the desserts I crave most often; I've made it so many times, I could do it blindfolded. This recipe creates a banana bread that is moist, melt-in-your-mouth tender, perfectly sweet, and aromatic. I tried pairing it with glazes, frostings, even butter. Turns out it doesn't need any of them. It's just that good on its own!

Neutral oil, for the loaf pan

3 medium (530g) soft, ripe, spotty bananas (see Note)

¾ cup packed (150g) light or dark brown sugar

2 large eggs

½ cup (113g) neutral oil, such as sunflower or grapeseed

1 tablespoon (14g) vanilla extract

1½ teaspoons (7g) distilled white vinegar

½ teaspoon (2g) kosher salt

½ teaspoon (1g) ground cinnamon

¼ teaspoon (0.5g) ground green cardamom (optional)

1½ cups (187g) all-purpose flour

½ teaspoon (3g) baking soda

½ teaspoon (2g) baking powder

2 tablespoons (30g) turbinado sugar (optional)

Flaky salt (optional; see Note)

Place an oven rack in the center of the oven. Preheat the oven to 350°F. Grease an 8 × 4-inch loaf pan with about 1 tablespoon neutral oil and line with parchment paper, letting any excess paper drape over the sides.

Peel the bananas. In a medium bowl, use a fork or a masher to mash the bananas until smooth. You should be left with about 1½ cups (400g) mashed bananas. Add the brown sugar, eggs, oil, vanilla, vinegar, salt, cinnamon, and cardamom (if using), and use a fork or whisk to combine.

Pile the flour, baking soda, and baking powder in a small mound on top of the wet ingredient mixture. Use a fork or whisk to gently combine just the dry ingredients by themselves. Then mix to fully incorporate into the batter, checking for any dry spots as you mix. Transfer the batter to the pan. Sprinkle the turbinado sugar and a little bit of flaky salt on top (if using).

Bake until a toothpick or cake tester comes out clean or with a few crumbs, about 1 hour. The banana bread should feel springy when gently tapped, not wobbly or liquid.

Let the banana bread cool completely in the pan, then lift the bread out using the parchment paper.

Notes:

• *Using spotty, ripe bananas is key to nailing the right sweetness level, since they have a higher sugar content than a spotless yellow-skinned banana. Letting them ripen on the counter is worth the wait.*

• *And while the turbinado sugar and flaky salt are optional, they're HIGHLY recommended. They add a pleasant crunch to each banana bread bite, so if it's not too much fuss, use them!*

Upside-Down Pineapple Coconut Cake

Makes one 10-inch cake | Prep Time: 25 minutes, plus 20 minutes chilling | Cook Time: 1 hour 10 minutes | Total Time: 1 hour 55 minutes

Initially inspired by piña colada flavors, this cake delivers a tender coconutty crumb with a caramelized, juicy pineapple mosaic on top. With every bite, the pineapple cubes explode in your mouth, releasing their tart and sweet flavor. It makes a great centerpiece for a birthday party, a bridal shower, an ending to a casual Wednesday-night dinner, or even a ridiculously decadent breakfast. The joy of flipping the cake upside down to reveal the pineapple pattern doesn't get old. Do it in front of your guests and watch their expressions—priceless!

Pineapple Topping

3 cups 1-inch cubed fresh pineapple (about 1 to 1¼ pounds; see Note)

1 cup (200g) granulated sugar

¼ cup (56g) rum or water

2 tablespoons (28g) fresh lemon juice

Coconut Cake

8 tablespoons (4 oz/113g) unsalted butter

1½ cups (140g) sweetened coconut flakes

1 cup packed (200g) dark brown sugar

1 cup (244g) heavy cream

1 tablespoon (13g) distilled white vinegar

1 tablespoon (14g) vanilla extract

1 teaspoon (3g) kosher salt

2 large eggs

1½ cups (185g) all-purpose flour

½ teaspoon (3g) baking soda

Vanilla ice cream, for serving (optional)

Make the pineapple topping: Line a 10-inch round cake pan or springform pan with parchment paper. Place the pan on a parchment-lined baking sheet. (This will catch any sugar drippings.) Arrange the pineapple in an even layer on the bottom of the pan.

In a medium saucepan (see Note), combine the sugar, rum, and lemon juice. Do not stir together, it will ruin the syrup! Set over medium heat and cover the saucepan with a lid. After 3 or 4 minutes, uncover and check that the sugar has dissolved and begun to darken. Cover and continue cooking undisturbed until the sugar turns amber brown, 2 to 3 minutes. Immediately and carefully pour the hot syrup over the pineapple, scraping the sides of the saucepan with a silicone spatula, being careful not to touch the hot syrup.

Make the coconut cake: Preheat the oven to 350°F.

Set the same medium saucepan over medium heat—no need to wash it or rinse off any caramelized sugar residue. Add the butter and cook until melted, 3 to 4 minutes. Add the coconut flakes and cook, stirring frequently, until the coconut is toasty, fragrant, and crisp, 3 to 4 minutes. Immediately remove the saucepan from the heat.

Whisk in the brown sugar, cream, vinegar, vanilla, and salt. The mixture should be warm, not hot, to the touch. (If it's still hot, set the mixture aside to cool for 5 to 10 minutes.) Add the eggs and whisk to combine.

Notes:

• If you don't feel like going out of your way to find a ripe pineapple (or babysit an unripe pineapple until the right time comes), canned pineapple will do the job. Frozen, then thawed pineapple cubes would also work. That said, fresh pineapple will have the best tartness level and texture out of all.

• We will be using this same saucepan for cake batter later, so make sure to grab a medium size, not a tiny one.

(recipe continues)

Pile the flour and baking soda in a little mound on top of the coconut mixture. Gently run your fingers or a whisk through the flour to evenly distribute the baking soda. Using a silicone spatula, mix until mostly smooth, checking for any hidden pockets of dry flour. Transfer the batter to the cake pan, pouring it right over the pineapple glaze.

Bake until the cake is golden brown, springy (but not wobbly), and a cake tester comes out clean or with a few crumbs, 50 to 55 minutes. Set aside to cool in the pan for 10 to 15 minutes.

Run a paring knife around the edge of the cake to help release it from the sides. Place a large serving plate over the cake pan and carefully flip, ending up with the plate at the bottom and the cake pan upside down on the plate. Remove the springform collar if you used one. Gently lift the pan off the cake and peel off the parchment paper to reveal the pineapple glaze. If any glaze has gathered in the middle of the cake, brush it toward the sides using a spatula or pastry brush. Let cool for 5 more minutes.

Slice and serve warm. Top with a scoop of vanilla ice cream, if you like.

Spiced Zucchini Cake
with Honey Cream Cheese Frosting

Makes one 8-inch loaf | Prep Time: 40 minutes | Cook Time: 1 hour 15 minutes | Total Time: 1 hour 55 minutes

Yes, this recipe has a million ingredients, and yes, it's still worth making: Juicy shreds of zucchini get swirled in a spiced cake batter for an inviting tenderness. While you can't taste the squash in the baked cake, you will certainly notice its textural presence. Sweetened with honey, the cake gets topped with a honey-laced cream cheese frosting, too! It's one of those cakes you can make on a Sunday night and grab a couple of slices every day to enjoy throughout the week. Pair it with coffee in the morning or hot tea.

Honey Zucchini Cake

Neutral oil, for the loaf pan

1 cup packed (200g) light or dark brown sugar

½ cup (113g) neutral oil, such as sunflower or grapeseed

½ cup (145g) honey

2 large eggs

2 tablespoons (9g) cocoa powder, sifted

1 tablespoon (6g) ground cinnamon

1 teaspoon (2g) ground ginger

½ teaspoon (1g) ground cardamom

¼ teaspoon (0.5g) ground cloves

¼ teaspoon (0.5g) ground nutmeg

1 teaspoon (6g) kosher salt

1 tablespoon (14g) vanilla extract

1 tablespoon (14g) distilled white vinegar

2¼ cups (285g) plus ¼ cup (30g) all-purpose flour

½ teaspoon (3g) baking soda

¼ teaspoon (1g) baking powder

12 ounces (350g) zucchini

Cream Cheese Frosting

4 ounces (113g) cream cheese, at room temperature

3 tablespoons (55g) honey

⅓ cup (37g) powdered sugar

⅛ teaspoon ground cinnamon, plus more for dusting

Kosher salt

Make the honey zucchini cake: Preheat the oven to 350°F. Grease an 8 × 4-inch loaf pan with a small amount of oil and line with parchment paper, letting the edges hang over the sides of the pan.

In a large bowl, combine the brown sugar, oil, honey, eggs, cocoa powder, cinnamon, ginger, cardamom, cloves, nutmeg, and salt. Vigorously whisk until the mixture looks frothy, 2 to 3 minutes. Add the vanilla and vinegar and whisk to combine.

Pile 2¼ cups (285g) of the flour in a mound right in the center of the batter. Add the baking soda and baking powder to the flour. Carefully whisk the dry ingredients using a dry whisk or fork to evenly distribute the rising agents throughout the flour. Using a silicone spatula, mix the dry ingredients and batter until combined (a few dry flour spots are okay at this point; make sure to not overmix).

Grate the zucchini on the coarse holes of a box grater. Measure out about 2 packed cups (350g) of grated zucchini and add to the cake batter. Sprinkle the zucchini with the remaining ¼ cup (30g) flour. Using a silicone spatula, fold the zucchini into the batter and mix until there are no more visible dry flour spots. Pour the cake batter in the loaf pan.

Bake until the cake is solid to the touch, springy (but not wobbly when tapped), and a cake tester or toothpick comes out clean or with a few crumbs, about 1 hour 15 minutes. Set aside to cool completely.

Make the cream cheese frosting: In a medium bowl, with an electric mixer or hand whisk, whisk the cream cheese, honey, powdered sugar, cinnamon, and a small pinch of salt until smooth and fluffy. It won't seem like a lot of frosting, but it's the perfect amount to cover the top of the cake and sweeten every bite.

Spread the frosting all over the cooled cake. Lightly dust cinnamon on top. Slice and serve.

Note: *If you don't feel like going out of the way and buying all the spices individually, substitute the spices in the recipe with 1½ tablespoons (10g) store-bought gingerbread or pumpkin spice mix.*

The Perfect Chocolate Cake

Makes one 9-inch square cake | Prep Time: 45 minutes | Cook Time: 55 minutes |
Total Time: 1 hour 40 minutes

Every Friday before Shabbat, this all-natural, all-organic, all-this, all-that store I go to for one thing only—amazing kombucha deals—would have a chocolate cake appear in the clearance area. One day, out of curiosity, I bought a $2 slice. Then bought it again, and again, and again. Despite feeling like I'm the only person buying it, since it was on sale nonstop, it had become one of my all-time favorite desserts. Finally one day, it tasted completely different—bland and dry. I assumed it was a one-time thing, but after giving it two more chances, it dawned on me: They changed the recipe.

I immediately started developing a recipe for the cake. After what felt like ages, I landed on a cake very reminiscent of the store-bought one: rich, chocolaty, and so tender. It's perfect for serving a crowd: Top it with fun sprinkles for children's birthdays or with edible flowers for an elegant centerpiece at your next gathering.

Chocolate Cake

Neutral oil, for the baking pan

1 cup (240g) heavy cream

1 tablespoon (14g) distilled white vinegar

1 cup (220g) neutral oil, such as sunflower or grapeseed

⅔ cup (70g) cocoa powder

1½ cups (300g) granulated sugar

1½ teaspoons (5g) kosher salt

⅓ cup (75g) lukewarm water

1 tablespoon (2g) instant espresso powder (optional; see Note)

2 large eggs

1⅔ cups (207g) all-purpose flour

1 teaspoon (5g) baking soda

Chocolate Buttercream

⅓ cup (35g) cocoa powder

⅓ cup (80g) heavy cream

12 tablespoons (6oz/170g) unsalted butter, at room temperature

½ teaspoon (3g) kosher salt

¾ cup (105g) powdered sugar, plus more if needed

2 to 4 tablespoons (26g to 52g) liquor of choice, such as rum or bourbon (optional)

Make the chocolate cake: Preheat the oven to 350°F. Lightly oil a 9-inch square pan. Line with parchment paper, letting the ends hang over the sides of the pan.

In a small bowl, stir together the cream and vinegar. Set aside.

In a medium saucepan (see Note), combine the oil and cocoa powder and heat over medium heat, whisking constantly, until the mixture is smooth and has a rich, dark brown color, 2 to 3 minutes. Remove the saucepan from the heat.

Add the sugar and salt to the pan and whisk to combine. Add the cream mixture and whisk until smooth. Add the lukewarm water and espresso powder (if using) and whisk again until smooth. Add the eggs and whisk until incorporated.

Pile the flour and baking soda in a little mound on top of the cocoa mixture. Gently run your fingers or a whisk through the dry ingredients to evenly distribute the baking soda. Using a wooden spoon or silicone spatula, fold in the flour, mixing until mostly smooth, checking for any hidden pockets of dry flour. Transfer the batter to the cake pan.

Bake until the cake is solid, springy (but not wobbly), and a cake tester comes out clean (a few crumbs on the cake tester are okay, just make sure there is no raw cake batter), 40 to 45 minutes. Set aside to cool in the pan.

Notes:

• The espresso powder must be instant for it to dissolve in the batter; ground coffee won't work as a substitute.

• We will be using this same saucepan for cake batter later, so make sure to grab a medium size, not a tiny one.

(recipe continues)

Make the chocolate buttercream: In a small saucepan, whisk together the cocoa and cream. Heat over medium heat, whisking occasionally, until the mixture forms a dark brown, slightly dry, crumbly glaze, about 2 minutes.

Scrape the cocoa mixture into a medium bowl, spreading it around the bowl to cool completely. Add 4 tablespoons (57g) of the butter and the salt and use an electric mixer or hand whisk to combine. Add ¾ cup (105g) of the powdered sugar, the liquor (if using), and the remaining 8 tablespoons (113g) butter and whisk until combined. Taste and add more powdered sugar as needed; I like to stop at ¾ cup (105g) , but for a sweeter tooth, you can add additional ¼ to ½ cup, to taste.

At this point, you can stop right here with this rich, velvety frosting. Or, to step it up a little, you can whip the buttercream for a light, airy consistency. To whip the buttercream, add a bunch of ice and a little bit of water to a large bowl. Set the buttercream bowl in the ice water (making sure no water gets in the buttercream) and use a whisk to whip the buttercream over the ice bath. Whip until the frosting is even lighter in color and cool to the touch.

Lift the cake out of the pan using the parchment paper and place on a serving platter. Frost the cake with the buttercream, slice, and serve.

No-Churn Salted Honey Lemon Ice Cream

Serves 6 to 8 | Prep Time: 10 minutes, plus 8 hours chilling | Total Time: 8 hours 10 minutes

Owning an ice cream machine was my dream since I was little, till I ended up buying one as an adult. Guess how many times I've used it? Once. I've used it once.

The great news is that no ice cream machine is needed to whip up this super-easy, no-churn, salted honey lemon number. While nine times out of ten I'd rather buy ice cream from a store, sometimes a special flavor combo makes homemade ice cream worth my time.

½ cup (100g) granulated sugar

3 tablespoons (18g) grated lemon zest (about 6 small lemons)

1 cup (235g) fresh lemon juice, plus more for serving

½ cup (145g) honey, plus more for serving

2 teaspoons (6g) kosher salt

2 cups (470g) heavy cream

Flaky salt, for serving

Lemon twists, for serving

In a freezer-safe medium container, combine the sugar and lemon zest and rub them together using your fingers until the sugar turns a pale-yellow and is deeply fragrant, about 2 minutes. (Lemon zest is packed with delicious natural oils, and the abrasive texture of sugar helps us extract most of that flavor.)

Add the lemon juice, honey, and kosher salt and stir, using a silicone spatula or wooden spoon, until most of the sugar has dissolved. Stir in the cream. Cover and freeze until the ice cream is firm and scoopable, at least 8 hours, preferably overnight.

To serve, let the ice cream sit at room temperature for 5 minutes. Scoop into serving glasses and top with a drizzle of honey and a sprinkle of flaky salt. If you're like me and you like your sour things *sour*, squeeze a lemon directly over the ice cream for a tangy kick. Twist a lemon peel over the ice cream (similar to what you would do to a cocktail) to release the lemony oils all over the ice cream.

Note: *If you have leftovers, this ice cream makes a really lovely sundae: Scoop the ice cream into serving bowls, top with crushed meringue or graham crackers for some crunch, a dollop of whipped cream, and a hefty drizzle of honey.*

Brown Butter Espresso Chocolate Chip Cookies

Makes 12 to 14 cookies | Prep Time: 25 minutes, plus 1 hour chilling | Cook Time: 12 minutes | Total Time: 1 hour 37 minutes

My move to the US introduced me to a cookie-loving culture I wasn't prepared for. Besides Oreos or a melt-in-your-mouth butter cookie, cookies have always been irrelevant on my list of dessert interests, but I finally developed a cookie I can't get enough of. I'm talking about a rich, crisp-but-fudgy cookie with so much depth of flavor. The cookie dough starts with nutty, toasty browned butter, a dash of instant espresso to bring out those chocolaty notes, dark brown sugar for a deep toffee-like flavor, and of course, crunchy salt flakes. Imagine starting your morning with these cookies, freshly baked, dipped in coffee—A DREAM.

12 tablespoons (6 oz/170g) unsalted butter

3 tablespoons (7g) instant espresso powder (see Note)

1 teaspoon (5g) distilled white vinegar

¾ cup packed (150g) dark brown sugar

⅓ cup (65g) granulated sugar

1 large egg

2 tablespoons (30g) sour cream or whole-milk yogurt

½ teaspoon (3g) kosher salt

1½ cups (185g) all-purpose flour

¼ teaspoon (1g) baking powder

⅛ teaspoon baking soda

½ cup (80g) semisweet chocolate chips or discs, plus more to taste

Flaky salt, for finishing (optional)

Note: *Make sure to use instant espresso powder; ground coffee will not work in this scenario.*

In a medium saucepan, heat the butter over medium. Cook, stirring occasionally, until the solids in the butter (you'll see them swirling around the bottom of the pan) become a nutty brown shade and the butter is nutty and fragrant, 6 to 8 minutes. Remove the pan from the heat and set it aside on a cool surface.

In a medium bowl, whisk together the espresso powder and vinegar until the espresso powder has dissolved. Add the brown sugar, granulated sugar, egg, sour cream, and kosher salt and whisk until smooth. Add the warm brown butter and whisk until combined. Note that the batter might look weirdly separated at first, but it will eventually emulsify and you'll be left with a silky, gooey batter.

Pile the flour, baking powder, and baking soda in a mound right on top of the batter. Use a fork, dry whisk, or just your fingers to gently combine the dry ingredients and evenly distribute the rising agents throughout the flour. Using a silicone spatula or wooden spoon, stir the dry ingredients into the batter until well combined, keeping an eye out for any pockets of dry flour. Fold in the chocolate chips or discs.

Cover the bowl and refrigerate for at least 1 hour, up to overnight, or until the cookie dough is easy to scoop and has a consistency similar to mashed potatoes. (If chilled overnight, allow the cookie dough to rest at room temperature for 30 to 45 minutes before baking, until easier to scoop.)

Preheat the oven to 350°F. Line one large or two standard baking sheets with parchment paper.

Using a 2-tablespoon ice cream scoop, scoop the cold dough and place it on the baking sheet, leaving about 2 inches of space between cookies. (If you're using a larger scoop, leave more room between cookies, as they will spread!)

Bake until fragrant, just set on the edges, with a soft center, 10 to 12 minutes.

Remove from the oven and hit the baking sheet with cookies on the counter to create a ripple effect in the cookies. Sprinkle with flaky salt (if using) and let them cool on the pan for 3 to 5 minutes. Enjoy the cookies warm.

Cremeş (Silky Vanilla Custard Slice)

Serves 12 | Prep Time: 20 minutes, plus 6 hours chilling | Cook Time: 40 minutes | Total Time: 7 hours

Ask any of my cousins, aunts, or uncles what dessert always brought us together, they'll all have the same answer: *cremeş* (pronounced creh-mesh). Our guests would request this dessert when visiting, every single time. At its core, this Austro-Hungarian delicacy is a slice of vanilla custard sandwiched between flaky puff pastry. It has as many names—Cremeschnitte in Germany, krémes in Hungary, kremówka in Poland—as it has different variations.

I've made it countless times, ever since I was a teen, some results more humbling than others. It's such a dear-to-my-heart recipe and I'm so stoked to share it with you.

Flaky Pastry

All-purpose flour, for dusting

1 pound frozen puff pastry, thawed overnight in the fridge

Vanilla Custard

6 cups (1,500g) whole milk

1 vanilla bean or 2 teaspoons (9g) vanilla extract

6 large egg yolks

1½ cups (300g) granulated sugar

½ teaspoon (3g) kosher salt

1 cup (120g) cornstarch (see Note)

12 tablespoons (6 oz/170g) cold unsalted butter, cubed

Powdered sugar, for serving

Note: *If you have a scale, now's the time to use it. If you don't have a scale, know that cornstarch is one of those ingredients that tends to clump together, so give it a gentle whisk and level your measuring cup. Just make sure your cup isn't heaping; you don't want to add more cornstarch than needed. Less is better in this case!*

Prepare the flaky pastry: Preheat the oven to 400°F. Line a baking sheet with parchment paper.

Dust a work surface with flour. The puff pastry will either come as two ½-pound sheets or one large 1-pound sheet. If the pastry isn't cut, slice the puff pastry in half so you're working with ½ pound of pastry at a time. Wrap one half in plastic wrap and return it to the fridge to keep cold.

Roll the other half of the pastry into a roughly 10 × 14-inch rectangle. (The measurements don't need to be super exact at this point; we'll trim the pastry later.) Lay the rolled-out pastry on the baking sheet and use a fork to poke small holes all over the pastry. Place another sheet of parchment on top, followed by another baking sheet to weight it down.

Bake until the pastry is a rich, amber color, 16 to 20 minutes. If your oven runs warm, check the pastry after 12 minutes, as this type of dough will brown fast. Remove the top baking sheet and parchment paper. Carefully transfer the pastry and parchment paper to a wire rack. Set aside to cool.

Place a new sheet of parchment on the bottom baking sheet and repeat the process with the remaining pastry sheet. Set aside to cool.

Set one of the baked pastry sheets on top of a deep 9 × 13-inch baking pan. Save the remaining pastry sheet for later. Using your fingers, gently work the pastry flat into the bottom of the pan, breaking off any edges as needed. This will be the base. Reserve any flaky scraps in a bowl.

Make the vanilla custard: Pour the milk into a large saucepan. If using a vanilla bean, split the pod and scrape the seeds into the milk. If not, add the vanilla extract. Bring the mixture to a gentle simmer over medium heat, whisking constantly to keep the milk from scorching. Remove the pan from the heat.

(recipe continues)

In a large bowl, whisk together the yolks, granulated sugar, and salt until smooth. Add a splash of the warm milk to the mixture to make things easier to combine. Add the cornstarch and whisk until combined. Whisking constantly and vigorously, slowly add ½ cup (125g) of the milk mixture. Repeat, whisking constantly, until you have added 4 cups of milk total (1,000g) and until the mixture in the bowl feels warm to the touch.

Set a fine-mesh strainer over the saucepan of milk. Pour the yolk/milk mixture through the fine-mesh strainer, into the saucepan. This will catch any potential cooked egg yolk bits.

Return the pan to medium heat. Begin whisking, staying close to the pan until the custard thickens. For the first 6 to 10 minutes, it will feel like nothing has changed: The mixture will feel liquid and look foamy. After 2 to 3 more minutes, the foam on top of the mixture will start to disappear. Reduce the heat to medium-low. Keep whisking! After another few minutes, the foam will subside and you'll see the first bubble. Keep whisking! The custard will start vigorously bubbling. Continue whisking for 1 to 2 minutes; the custard will thicken and become harder to stir. It will be smooth and thick, a bit like mayonnaise, consistency-wise. Remove the pan from the heat.

Add 2 tablespoons (28g/1 oz) of the butter to the custard and whisk until incorporated. Repeat with another 2 tablespoons of butter. Repeat until all the butter has been added.

Using a clean fine-mesh strainer, pour the hot custard over the pastry base in the 9 × 13-inch pan. Use a spatula to evenly spread it out.

Crumble the reserved baked pastry sheet over the custard, including any scraps reserved from making the base. Place the pan in the refrigerator to let the custard set for at least 6 hours, preferably overnight, until firm.

Right before serving, dust the pastry with powdered sugar. Slice and serve.

Upside-Down Orange Cardamom Olive Oil Cake

Makes one 10-inch round cake or 9-inch square cake | Prep Time: 1 hour 10 minutes | Cook Time: 1 hour | Total Time: 2 hours 10 minutes

Imagine a layer of slowly simmered oranges in cardamom sugar, wrapped around a soft olive oil cake. Olive oil in a cake might seem like an odd choice, but its bright sharpness brings such a memorable, unique flavor to any dessert, and a level of moisture that will have you coming back for more. Flavored with floral cardamom and sugar-rubbed orange zest, the cake gets better and better as it sits at room temperature. It's one of my most loved recipes for a reason, and I am so excited to see your version of it.

If you're feeling frisky and want to try other citrus options, most oranges will work, from blood oranges to mandarin oranges to Cara Caras. Meyer lemons are also a great alternative, especially with a sprinkle of sugar mixed with citric acid, for some extra tang. Limes, on the other hand, will get a little too bitter.

Candied Oranges

3 medium oranges, gently scrubbed

1¼ cups (250g) sugar

5 green cardamom pods, crushed, or 1 teaspoon (2g) ground cardamom

Orange Cardamom Olive Oil Cake

Extra-virgin olive oil, for the baking pan and oranges

1⅓ cups (266g) sugar

2 tablespoons (8g) grated orange zest (about 2 oranges)

12 cardamom pods, freshly ground and pods removed, or 2 teaspoons (4g) ground cardamom

½ teaspoon (3g) kosher salt

4 large eggs

¾ cup (155g) extra-virgin olive oil, plus more for serving

¼ cup (56g) fresh orange juice (about 1 medium orange)

1 teaspoon (5g) vanilla extract

2 cups (250g) all-purpose flour

1 teaspoon (4g) baking powder

¼ teaspoon (1g) baking soda

Make the candied oranges: Using a sharp knife, cut the oranges into ⅛-inch-thick slices. (Reserve the orange ends and any thicker slices cut by mistake for snacking or juicing.) Store the orange slices in a medium bowl.

In a medium saucepan, combine 1¼ cups (315g) water, the sugar, and the cardamom, swirling to combine. Cut a parchment paper round slightly smaller than the diameter of the saucepan and cut a small hole in the middle. This is called a cartouche (parchment paper lid). Add the oranges to the pan and place the cartouche right on top, making sure it touches the oranges. This will keep them submerged in the liquid while simmering.

Bring the mixture to a boil over medium heat. Reduce the heat to medium-low and simmer until the orange rind is softened and the pith is less opaque, 40 to 50 minutes. Remove the pan from the heat.

Meanwhile, make the orange cardamom olive oil cake: Preheat the oven to 350°F. Brush a 10-inch round cake pan or springform pan or a 9-inch square pan with olive oil. Line the bottom and the sides of the pan with parchment paper and brush with a little more oil. Line a baking sheet with parchment paper and place the cake pan on the baking sheet; this will catch any potential sugar drippings.

In a medium bowl, combine the sugar, orange zest, cardamom, and salt. Rub them together using your fingers until the mixture is pale yellow and fragrant. Add the eggs and vigorously whisk until the mixture becomes light, fluffy, and pale, 4 to 5 minutes by hand or 2 to 3 minutes if using an electric mixer. Constantly whisking, slowly stream in the olive oil. Add the orange juice and vanilla and whisk to combine.

(recipe continues)

In a small bowl, whisk together the flour, baking powder, and baking soda. Using a silicone spatula, gently fold the dry ingredients into the wet ingredients, making sure to incorporate any dry patches into the batter. Arrange the syrupy orange slices on the bottom of the cake pan, creating a scallop pattern. Instead of going in circles around the cake, overlap the orange slices into straight lines. Try not to leave gaps in between orange slices as the cake batter will seep through. Repeat until the base of the pan is fully covered in orange slices. Arrange any remaining slices around the edges of the pan. Drizzle 2 tablespoons of the cardamom orange syrup over the orange layer, and lightly drizzle the oranges with 2 tablespoons of olive oil (see Note). Carefully pour the cake batter over the orange slices.

Bake, checking on the cake after about 30 minutes. If the cake seems to be browning fast on top, cover with foil and continue baking. Bake until the cake is solid, springy (but not wobbly), and a cake tester comes out clean (a few crumbs are okay; just make sure there is no raw cake batter on the cake tester), 30 to 45 minutes longer. All ovens are a little different, hence the roomy time range.

Let the cake cool for 10 minutes in the pan.

Place a large serving plate over the cake pan and carefully flip, ending up with the plate at the bottom and the cake pan upside down on the plate. Remove the springform collar if you used one. Gently lift the pan off the cake and peel off the parchment paper to reveal the orange pattern.

Brush some of the reserved orange cardamom syrup on top of the cake and drizzle more olive oil on top. Slice and serve.

Note: *You will be left with quite a bit of orange cardamom syrup. Don't throw it away! Strain the syrup into a deli container or jar, date it, label it, and store it in the fridge. Mix it with seltzer and lemon or lime juice for a refreshing bev, or save it for any future cocktail opportunities.*

ACKNOWLEDGMENTS

Hashem, thank you for blessing me with the gift of sharing my love of food with your creation. Thank you for giving me the courage to pursue this and create my little world.

To my community, I am so grateful for all your pictures, videos, emails, and texts of you sharing my recipes with your loved ones or by yourself. It's a blessing to be a part of your world, and I'm so grateful to have you. Every recipe I write has you in mind, so thank you for always asking questions, staying curious, and making my recipes better. Thank you, thank you, thank you!

To my mother, thank you for nurturing this never-ending curiosity of being in the kitchen, watching cooking shows with me, thrifting for props, and going out of your way to buy everything I needed for my cooking experiments. Even if our resources were so tight, you somehow found a way to make things happen. Thank you for always supporting me, even if you didn't understand what I was doing. And also for holding the umbrella to diffuse the light while shooting on our tiny balcony, in the freezing cold winter or in the middle of a hot summer day. Sorry, I had fewer calls with you while working on this cookbook. Mulțumesc mama!

And to my father, who also doesn't exactly understand what I'm doing, thank you for sacrificing your time to provide for your family and teaching me to be cautious, find humor in everything, breathe, relax, and always remind me where I came from. Köszi papa!

Nicole Tourtelot, thank you for believing there's something worth exploring in my work and giving me the confidence to pursue this massive project. Thank you for showing me the value of my work and answering all my anxious calls with your calmness. I'm very grateful to you.

Jenn Sit, you were the first to call about the possibility of writing a book when I was in Romania while immigrating. The thought of a book felt so farfetched then. I'm so grateful for your patience and you waiting for me to settle in the US. I feel so lucky we got to work together on my first cookbook. Thank you for your trust, constant guidance, and help, for encouraging me to be bolder and more confident in my writing, creating a safe space, and welcoming all my silly questions. I couldn't have done this without you!

Jeanelle Olson, thank you for bearing with me and my ridiculously late emails with dozens of recipes for review. Thank you for asking all the right questions when testing these recipes; you've taught me so much!

Katie Wayne, thank you for making the cookbook shoot go so smoothly, from ordering everything we possibly needed, to nonstop schlepping giant duffel bags to the shoot, to letting us use your strawberry-masking-tape-wrapped tools, to creating the game plan for shooting 100 recipes and pulling a genuine laugh out of me in the cover photo. Without you, this shoot wouldn't have been as smooth! I am so grateful for your talent and ridiculously fun playlists.

James Tenenhouse, you are hilarious; thank you for making my jaw hurt daily from all the laughter on shoot. I'm so glad you flew from London for this. I'm so honored this was the first cookbook shoot you've worked on, I couldn't have asked for a better person to cook these recipes. Thank you for asking all the right questions and handling my stuffy-cutting instructions. You have made these recipes so much better and more approachable; I hope you work 100 more cookbook shoots. It was such a joy to work with you, thank you for being such a gem!

Maeve Sheridan, I am so grateful for your colorful spirit and excellent team. Thank you for curating such a wonderful collection of dishes and understanding my vision, from sourcing Romanian plates to dishes with Hungarian motifs to those eyeball plates we could never use. I am so thankful for your warmth and guidance throughout the shoot, thank you for making the process so seamless. I miss drinking lattes out of the cutest little props of yours. Sorry for staining your turquoise pan with turmeric!!!

Nico Schinco, thank you! I have never worked with someone who maneuvers light quite like you. I could tell you, "I want this photo to feel like you're on a patio in August at seven p.m. watching the sunset," and you'd somehow manage to capture that exact feel. Thank you for bearing with my hundreds of "Can we get a close-up shot?" I am so grateful for your talent; thank you for bringing these recipes to life in such a beautiful way. I don't think I'll ever get tired of staring at these wonderful photos.

Nikki Jessop, I gasped when I saw how beautiful you made the recipes look; they were so symmetrical, neat, and precise in form and shape. Without you, I wouldn't have that perfect cabbage roll cake or those perfectly coated bourekas! Thank you for making these recipes more beautiful than I could have and introducing us to your precious little puppy!

Francis Lam, thank you for making the whole process much more attainable! I appreciate our chats guiding me through all the book-making steps.

Becky Hughes, you were the first to see something in my work, and I'm beyond grateful. Thank you for your trust and for helping me refine my eye and filming skills. Natasha Janardan, thank you for the salt and pepper shakers—I'm still not over them—and for making my videos so much better.

Patrick Moynihan, I'm so appreciative you noticed something in my work good enough to give me an opportunity at Food52; thank you for your kindness and constant involvement, from being there for me at my first live to your kind comments on every post. And to the greater Food52 team, thank you for letting me share my recipes with your community.

Note: Page references in italics indicate photographs.

Copyright © 2024 by Gelen Media LLC
Photographs copyright © 2024 by
Nico Schinco

All rights reserved.

Published in the United States by Clarkson
Potter/Publishers, an imprint of the Crown
Publishing Group, a division of Penguin
Random House LLC, New York.
ClarksonPotter.com

CLARKSON POTTER is a trademark and
POTTER with colophon is a registered
trademark of Penguin Random House LLC.

Library of Congress Cataloging-in-
Publication Data
Names: Gelen, Carolina, author. | Schinco,
Nico, photographer.
Title: Pass the plate : 100 delicious, highly
shareable, everyday recipes / Carolina
Gelen ; photographs by Nico Schinco.
Description: New York : Clarkson Potter/
Publishers, [2024] | Includes index. |
Identifiers: LCCN 2023052026 | ISBN
9780593581872 (hardcover) | ISBN
9780593581889 (epub)
Subjects: LCGFT: Cookbooks.
Classification: LCC TX714 .G442 2024 |
DDC 641.5—dc23/eng/20240228
LC record available at
https://lccn.loc.gov/2023052026

ISBN 978-0-593-58187-2
Ebook ISBN 978-0-593-58188-9

Printed in China

Editor: Jennifer Sit
Editorial assistant: Elaine Hennig
Designer: Ian Dingman
Production editor: Patricia Shaw
Production manager: Jessica Heim
Compositors: Merri Ann Morrell and
    Nick Patton
Food stylist: Kaitlin Wayne
Food stylist assistants: James Tenenhouse
    and Nikki Jessop
Prop stylist: Maeve Sheridan
Prop stylist assistants: Zach Molina and
    Tsering Dolma
Photo assistants: Michael Carnevale and
    Angelina Troia
Copy editor: Kate Slate
Proofreaders: Karen Ninnis, Robin Slutzky,
    Sigi Nacson, and Nancy Inglis
Indexer: Elizabeth T. Parson
Publicist: Natalie Yera-Campbell
Marketer: Stephanie Davis

10 9 8 7 6 5 4 3 2 1

First Edition